Patricia Iris

Viva Voce

The Living Voice

Disclaimer

This book is intended to share basic VIVA voice-work for personal use. The techniques are simple and easy to learn. However, you, the reader, must assume responsibility for your own emotional, physical and spiritual welfare. Please use your common sense at all times. If in doubt seek the help of a qualified VIVA practitioner.

The author and publishers disclaim any liability arising directly or indirectly from the use of this book and take no responsibility whatsoever for your actions or the outcome of any VIVA treatment administered by you, on yourself or others.

First Edition Printed August 2007

Published by
New Vision Media LLP

www.newvisionmedia.co.uk

ISBN 978-0-9549222-5-2

Printed and bound in the UK by T.J. International
Padstow, Cornwall

Contents

Introduction

Welcome to Viva Voce – The Living Voice. In this book I intend to introduce you to the miraculous healing voice that you possess and how it can accelerate your ascension and balance your earthly existence.

First of all, a little about how I came to this point in my life.

It has been my great honour and privilege to have been gifted a beautiful voice, which over the years I have used successfully as a singer, speaker, teacher and healer. I know that my voice has a healing quality to it, and I have used it as guided, when needed.

In November 2006, Archangel Michael, the Archangel with special responsibility for the throat chakra asked me, during a meditation, to write this book and develop a series of workshops to help humanity find their voice once again, move from discord to harmony, from descension to ascension.

Viva Voce is my first book and I hope you will find the content of interest and use, because it is only by using the tools for transformation contained herein that the transition to higher vibration will take place. Using the voice is my chosen path to Ascension, there are of course many paths, hopefully, you, like me, will enjoy using and developing your voice for this purpose.

I have been blessed by the presence of Archangels Michael, Gabriel, Raphael, Uriel and Metatron, as I have been writing. For their presence and their words of Divine wisdom, I am exceedingly grateful.

I am also very grateful to my wonderful, loving husband, Bill Kerins, who has supported me throughout this effort in every way possible. Most importantly, giving me the freedom, time and space to bring the book forward by generating the income to live, while I do so.

Amazing Earth angels have been instrumental too in encouraging and helping me to bring this information to you. I give them all my heartfelt thanks.

The essence of this book and all therein is simplicity, there seems to be a great desire in humanity to make life complicated and a struggle. Simply using your own voice in conscious ways can, and will, open the doorways to other experiences, dimensions, universes and vibrations of life. They await you now, as this moment, is the time you agreed, a long time ago, to open this book, read and digest its contents. Be open, be like a sponge, absorbing only that which feels right for you at this point in your journey.

In the opening chapters I set out my stall of what I believe makes us all multi-vibrational beings and how vibration works. You will, however, arrive at a point where your self-work begins.

Be prepared with journal and pen, an open mind, and a wonderful box of tissues, ready to undertake some transformational work.

You may prefer to read the entire book through first and then come back to the exercises however you need to be honest with yourself at this stage, would you take the time to do that or not?

Whatever you choose to do, please enjoy this book and prepare to Find your Voice, your VIVA VOCE once again.

With Infinite Love and Blessings.

Patricia Iris

'Intention is a force in the Universe, and everything and everyone is connected to this invisible force',

Dr Wayne Dyer.
(Author of 'The Power of Intention').

Intention

BE

Be the change in your life
Be the start of the miracle
Be the love of your life
Be the star, the highest pinnacle

Be the power that's within
Be the chakras as they spin
Be at one with your Source
Be committed to stay the course

Be the friend you've always wanted
Be the lover you have courted
Be the child, God and Goddess within
Be the freedom and the forgiven

Be the peace and bliss
Of the silent Angel's shimmering kiss

Patricia Iris

My intention in Viva Voce is to share with you my current knowledge and understanding of what it is to be a multi-dimensional and multi-vibrational being at this time. I will share a variety of different exercises that will assist you in re-calibrating to a higher vibrational level, as well as a range of very simple voice healing techniques, guided and orchestrated by the Archangels.

Some of these techniques are being re–introduced to us from the days of Atlantis and Lemuria, when we were well used to using them. As you read and address the relevant exercises, Archangel Michael will also come through to resolve any issues that are present in your throat chakra energy field and transmute them to the Light. All of this is to assist you in your preparation for the 5th Dimension Ascension process.

As I announce my intention, I am acutely aware that I set into motion the Universe and Divine Intelligence, which is listening to my every word every thought. It is picking up the transmission, and sending it out all over the galaxy. Amazing things will begin to happen, and that is the way it is.

This book is not about me, although I have taken the time to let you know where I am coming from and my background and experience, so that you feel comfortable with that.

To some degree I feel this is an urgent message, needing to be heard, spoken and sung by billions of people NOW.

The time is NOW.

Background Information

There are many sound and vibration therapies available and sound healing techniques. I have studied with voice Masters, Jill Purce, Chris James, Tim Wheater and Frank Kane, all of whom have shared with me unique and different aspects of the voice and the use of sound. I have been using the tools that I will share with you for seven years. I have developed them, working with groups and individuals. I bring my own unique recipe to this, and that is one that includes the following ingredients.

My unique recipe

- A professionally trained singer with Neilson Taylor, RSAMD, Glasgow

- A Student of Louise L Hay, attending her workshops to advanced level and subsequently meeting her in San Diego at her home. I conducted many Louise Hay weekends from my home in the Highlands of Scotland.

- Diplomas in Hypnotherapy, psychotherapy and counselling.

- Advanced practitioner in Emotional Freedom Technique.

- Certification in Aura Soma Colour Work.

- Teacher of meditation, visualisation and toning.

- Reiki Master/ Teacher in Usui and Karuna with additional studies of the original Japanese Reiki and Kotodama.

- Angel Workshops with the Rev Andrew Hunter.

- Devotee of Angel divas, Doreen Virtue and Diana Cooper.

- Radio presenter on www.internetradio.co.uk - the Spiritual Matters programme.

As you can see, as a therapist and workshop facilitator, I have a wealth of 'tools' to call upon to help people during their process.

Evolution

My journey with sound as a healing modality started some 7 years ago – on the 5th May 2000, when I delivered, along with two colleagues, a sound workshop which offered:

- balancing the charkas
- sounding to raise energy levels
- learning to resonate with each other
- balance each other with sounds.

I went on to develop these workshops over the years. Archangel Michael guided me to call these workshops 'Find Your Voice'. I was very successful with these in Edinburgh, Inverness and around the country, as more and more men and women wanted to get to the root of their throat problems, enabling themselves to express the fullness of who they really are.

Archangel Michael asked me in November 2006 to completely revamp my workshop, give it a new name and add many different and new techniques to it. He wanted a structured approach, similar to that of Reiki as he felt participants would relate well to this.

Workbooks and CDs were to be made available. He wanted Master/Teachers to be 'out there' spreading the word or sound! He even went as far as to give me the name, VIBREIKI, which at first I thought was to be the name of the workshop however, it transpired that this was the energy that had been coming through my voice. It would continue to do so. Now they were naming it, so that I knew what the difference was when a certain tone is present in the voice. One way of describing that would be when I get out of my own way and allow myself to be sung or spoken.

VIVA was born when Archangel Michael gave me the information that the workshop would be called **V**ibration, **I**nner Healing, **V**oice-work with the **A**rchangels. Using the first letter of each word it spells **VIVA,** an acronym, my curiosity led me to look it up in the dictionary and VIVA, in its own right, means 'Long Life' or lively and vivacious, in the term VIVA VOCE, it means – The Living Voice.

I was, and still am very excited and honoured that I was chosen to manifest this powerful healing sound workshop. Very quickly, this new baby needed to be nourished and looked after, and like many of these metaphysical births, it all happened very quickly. I was to change my name, which coincided with me getting married. However, I was not to take up the name (professionally) of my husband, but rather to use my middle name, **Iris**.

The reason behind this being that the vibration of the name was much higher, and so Patricia Iris was born. Iris, according to Greek mythology was a loyal messenger of the Gods, and as I feel that I am a messenger of the Archangels, it feels right. But you know what they say, 'Don't shoot the messenger'.

The Archangels raised my vibration and altered my transmission, at a time which made me even more sensitive, and I have had to take stock of all my eating and drinking habits. Not that they were poor, they just needed adjusting and tweaking a bit.

I have been involved since the age of eleven with choirs, professional and amateur performance in opera, concert, musicals, and with bands. Added to that, running voice and vibration workshops and giving voice coaching. It seemed that all I had learned was to be integrated with my therapeutic skills in this new and exciting way for the greater good of humanity.

These wonderful Illumined Beings told me that a book must accompany and complement the workshops as soon as possible, to assist the healing, and instigate vibrational shifts in different ways. So here I am writing this in the knowledge that, as you read it, the Archangels and their extremely high vibrational field of consciousness are embracing you. The healing has already started, just take a moment to feel this, breathe in deeply, take it right to the base of your spine and then release and relax as you do so.

Having stated my intention loud and clear to the Universe that a book is now in progress, I awaited inspiration and motivation. The latter was a joy to observe, I became aware of a pattern of procrastination that I have had to work hard to overcome. As I peeled away the layers of procrastination, it became apparent that the real root of my challenge was fear. A fear of putting myself out there, of empowering as the feminine, because, in past lives, every time I had done this, I had in someway been stopped in my tracks. As a result, I had learned to play small and hide my innate knowledge and wisdom. I now know that this is my Karmic soul pattern, and in many ways writing this book has been a cathartic experience in identifying and dealing with that. I am glad to say that with lots of help from the Illumined realms and earth angels, this has been achieved and here I am, putting myself out there.

The Universe has responded to my set intention by bringing the information to me that I need to write about. This has happened in a variety of ways. Mostly, information has come at times of meditation, or times spent in nature whilst contemplating and reflecting, and simply being.

Like Diana the Huntress, I set my bow at my target and asked for help with focus. To my great surprise and honour, Kuthumi, one of the ascended masters came in to me to help with this.

He motivates and encourages with insistence and consistence. Words, such as persistence, being constantly drip fed into my psyche. Then, the wonderful realisation dawned that when I need help on any level, all I need to do is ask and it will be delivered.

Wobbly moments have occurred. However, help has come forward on request. Remaining in Trust and Faith that all would be well, has simply grown and grown as the book has grown, and taken on its own identity. Being aware of these negative times is half the battle, being able to address them so effectively is miraculous. Everything being in Divine right order, as always.

Synchronicity

Following my commitment to the book, doors began opening immediately. Synchronistically, a lady came in who had recently written a book. She is also a sound healer and works with the Hathors.

She pointed me in the direction of a publisher, whom she felt had integrity and would do the job competently. Interestingly another publisher appeared shortly after that, with a similar pedigree. Tuning in, and listening to my gut and the resonating energy between us, it felt right to go with the second one. Exercising my inner discernment I chose the right one for me.

I hope you, like me, will learn, from those kind of incidents, that the Universe will always offer us choices so that we can tune in, resonate with the vibration, then make the decision that feels right for us.

Message

My message is one of unconditional love. Most importantly, learning to love yourself to a degree that you probably can't even imagine as yet. Using the sound of your wondrous voice, with grace and integrity, will help you to do that. Singing with the Source of All that is, the song of creation, the song of joy through time and space.

'Every visible thing in the world
Is put in the charge of an Angel'

Saint Augustine

Archangels

I would like to share some information with you about the four main Archangels that I will be working with throughout the creation of this book. They have asked that I introduce some meditative work at this juncture, in preparation for what is to come. I have also included some of the many Earth Angels who have assisted me with their guidance for many years.

I am not sure exactly how long I have been consciously working with Archangels. When I started to work with Reiki, I always called forward the Angels of Love, Light and Healing. I was inspired by the quality of the energy they would bring to the proceedings. I called upon the power and presence of the Archangelic Realms to work with us, though not individually. There are thousands of them, even so, a distinct and different energy would surround us.

I began to invoke the power and presence of the Christ energy. This came in very definitely. A pronounced shift in my vibrational field would take place. Sensitive recipients would remark on the increase in energy flowing. Added to this, the power and presence of Mikao Usui, the Reiki Sensei, to do the attunements through me. Indeed, It was a powerful energy recipe.

Archangel Michael

The spiritual warrior angel began to make his presence felt, more and more, in my healing sessions. Under his tutelage, I learned how to deal with the negative entities that could be working through individuals. There were times when, side by side, we had a battle on our hands. However, the Light had already won, and with that Trust and Faith, all was very well.

Being a Spiritual Warrior can be testing at times and calling on Archangel Michael to work with you is a must.

Our connection strengthened and strengthened. I had never thought on myself as a channeler. However, this is what was happening. He was working through me and with me. I have very strong clairvoyance abilities, and this works through me when I am working with groups or individuals, allowing me to see and intuit on a high level.

Archangel Michael has an amazing blue cloak which I suggest you use for protection. His loyal luminous blue angels, who help clear and cleanse our healing work place, which exists on another dimension, are always present during my workshops and healing sessions.

His name means, 'He who is like God'. His field of consciousness is so great, that he can be working with millions of people at any one time. However, as the Universal Spiritual Laws dictate - ***he has to be asked!***

With his mighty sword, Archangel Michael has helped me with hundreds of clients. During guided visualisation, we invite in those we need to work with:

- to sever cords, (the ties that bind)
- to bring back our freedom
- to restore our confidence
- our self-esteem
- our courage and strength
- to retrieve our power.

He uses his mighty sword to sever those connectors or he may use his magnificent golden scissors to cut away the ties that bind and restrict. Some of the self-imposed limitations can look like bandages that have been strapped around people, forcing inertia and blockages into their lives.

He is the Archangel in charge of developing the Throat Chakra, the place of honest communication, truth and leadership. He clears away the past life traumas that we hold there. Strengthening our abilities to speak up and speak out,

without fear. He does this for individuals, and for the greater good of humanity as well.
So prepare to put yourself out there!

Some of us have old ancestral patterns of scarcity and lack playing through us. A feeling of not being enough. Archangel Michael works to remove that pattern and feeling from your entire energy blueprint, building your self-confidence and self-esteem.

Deep Royal Blue is the colour of a fully developed and functioning throat chakra. Wearing blue at your throat, if you have challenges with it, is a good idea.

Archangel Michael comes through on the 1st ray from Source or Mother/Father God, and this is the blue ray of power, will and protection. His element is fire, and he brings you the passionate willpower to achieve your goals and lead the way.

Tuesday, is the day that his energetic presence is the strongest, and as Divine Intelligence would have it, I am writing this section on (guess what, yes), a Tuesday!

If you want to be someone who can speak out and communicate with honesty, love and integrity, then working with and aligning your energy to Archangel Michael is a must.

Meditation and Invocation.

Let's just take a moment to invoke his presence formally, invocation being a particularly powerful thing to do, although I suspect you know he is here working with us already.

- Close your eyes and take a few deep breaths.

- Centre and align your body.

- Feel your sitting bones on the chair.

- Take your awareness to your feet and put your roots into the ground.

- Focus on your crown and see the beautiful connection you have to the Universe.

- Breathe in relaxation and love, breathe out relaxation and love.

- Say out loud, 'I invoke the power and presence of Archangel Michael to be with me, to stand beside me to strengthen and protect me, my family, my home and my possessions.

Do this three times - with feeling.

As your every inner thought is being listened to, you must have complete faith that this protection is in place, as any negative thought or worry will negate the process requested. There is no point in asking for help if you are not going to believe it is forthcoming.

Gently bring yourself back into the room, open your eyes and stretch every muscle, take your hands as high as they will go above your head, and point your toes down to the earth. Stretch them out as far as they will go.

What did you notice? Take your journal and note down the sensations and feelings you experienced, perhaps you felt Angel wings stroke your face or touch your hair, note it all down for future reference.

Archangel Gabriel

His name means 'God is my strength', he is another co-creator of VIVA – VOCE. He has been a 'force majeure' in my life, as he is one of my guides.

He is in charge of the element of water, and as a Piscean, I have a natural and deep connection with him. With him prodding me along for some considerable time now, I have a number of creative projects underway, this book being only one of them. Gabriel brings order out of chaos and spiritual and physical discipline into your life when asked. He is all about purification, clarity, grace, hope and guidance.

Interestingly, one of the theatrical roles I have often been called upon to perform is that of the Archangel Gabriel, in an outdoor rendition of The Nativity play. (Directed by John Claudius my front cover artist). The spotlight would alight on me as I appeared in the trees, about 40 feet up in the air, on scaffolding where I was required to sing to the shepherds below, freezing cold with ice underfoot.

The scaffolding was an improvement on the fork lift truck they started out with. It proved to be too noisy and emitted the most ghastly fumes that would have asphyxiated me, the shepherds and the sheep given half a chance! It was all very authentic and entertaining but please don't try it at home!

Fortunately, the real Archangels wouldn't feel the chill of the Scottish Highland winter!.

I have found that asking Archangel Gabriel to help me with clarity in particular, has made it easier for me to let go of my past in this lifetime. It has helped me make clear decisions and then, of course, having done that, closed the old doors, the wonderful new doors have been given the freedom and space to open.

From a purification point of view he helps you with powerful ways to cleanse yourself of negative emotions and thoughts, and also helps you on a physical level to detoxify your body.

As I have been writing this and checking it over, I realise that the clear message here is to **Ask, Ask**, **Ask** your angels for help - and it will come!

Let's take a few moments to connect with Archangel Gabriel who has just whispered this lovely message to me

Learn to know Yourself
Believe in Yourself
Believe in your Dream
Believe in Truth and Love

Thank you Gabriel for these wonderful words.

Meditation and Invocation

Take sacred space by being where you will not be disturbed for about 20 minutes. Light a candle, inviting the Light in as you do so. Make yourself comfortable sitting on a chair or on a couch or on the floor in a Yoga position whatever is right for you, is just fine.

Take your awareness to your breathing.

Notice how the breath feels cool as it enters your nose and when you exhale it has warmed up slightly.

Take a few breaths to conduct this observation, making sure that you are breathing right down to your pubic bone before allowing the breath to come up and release.

Let go of any tension in your neck and shoulders by simply saying,' I am freeing my neck, I am freeing my shoulders, I am freeing each and every muscle in my body.'

Good, that's right, just allow that warm glow of relaxation fill your body.

Your awareness is moving to your inner screen in your mind's eye, you see your heart clearly, it looks like a wonderful cave and you make your way into it, right to the back.

There is a stairway going down to a lower level and you make your way down there now, accompanied by your Guardian Angel and Guides, who are always with you.

There is an air of expectant excitement as you glide down to the last step and make your way to a beautiful doorway.

Going through the door you see ahead of you, a lovely garden and a seat where you sit down.

You are comfortable and relaxed. Now, repeat the following invocation, three times.

"I invoke the power and presence of Archangel Gabriel to be with me now. Please bless me with your pure white ray and fill my four-body energy field with it. I ask that all symbols of my Divine Purpose be illuminated now, to attract in all the help I need to accomplish my goals. Gabriel. Please bring grace, joy, clarity, understanding and generosity of Spirit into my life. I ask for your guidance as to how I should proceed on my sacred journey".

Be prepared to see, hear or feel the presence of Archangel Gabriel and his pure white light.

Listen and focus on the stillness of your breath.

Listen, and don't edit what comes in and yes, it might sound like your own voice and that is OK.

It might be a very distinctive voice and that is OK, it may be a gut feeling that you get.

When you feel this process is complete thank Archangel Gabriel and he will silently disappear.

Come back up the staircase and return to the stillness of your breathing. When you are ready, return to the room. Stretch, open your eyes and reconnect with this beautiful Universe.

The answers may come to you loud and clear in the hours and days to come as Archangel Gabriel and the Universe speak loudly to you, through signs along the way. By that I mean, noticing what comes on the radio when you switch it on, the first few words of a song or a programme on TV or an article that you happen to see or a book falling off a shelf. You will know, it will hold meaning for you, it will resonate with your vibration. Be open and receptive. He may have given you information in the here and now, if so write it down.

Take your journal and pen and write down the messages, images or impressions that you were given for future reference. What doesn't make sense just now may make a lot of sense in the days to come.

Archangel Raphael

Raphael is a wonderful Archangel known for his healing and abundance, not forgetting his amazing pink salve, the 'Savlon' of the Angelic Healing world. He is associated with the third eye and all the 'clairs' e.g. clairvoyance, clairsentience, clairaudience and claircognisance. He works with you during healing sessions and assists Archangel Michael on entity releasing jobs by clearing and cleansing the healee afterwards - restoring their balance and equilibrium. He stitches up the Aura and uses the pink salve to heal where the stitches have been inserted, to heal the breached area.
Raphael empowers the emerald ray, the fifth ray which brings us beauty, harmony and balance.

Invoke his presence when needing assistance during sound healing sessions, in fact any type of energy healing. However, because his element is air, he is particularly potent in sound healing and when communicating, facilitating and training. Call in his energy to protect you and care for you when you go off on your travels as well.

A powerful invocation to use is:

"I invoke the power and presence of Archangel Raphael of the emerald ray to be with me now. I ask him to empower my third eye and fill me with love, healing, abundance and Light. Please be with me on my sacred journey through life, especially on my travels around this planet."

Archangel Raphael facilitates the shift from poverty thinking to abundance thinking. Call him in to remind you of who you really are - a Divine aspect of God and Goddess, and allow him to help you with your cosmic ordering.

Affirmation:

"The Universe always provides for me in every abundant and prosperous way, and so it is. Thank you Universe!"
Creative Visualisation.

Take sacred space.

Take your awareness to your breathing, monitor it closely.

Focus on your heart centre and see it open before you into a beautiful cavern.

Invoke the power and presence of Archangel Raphael to be with you, and stand beside you, do this three times and observe as he appears bathed in his magnificent emerald green robes.

Now, sit down at the desk provided in your heart space, take a pen and paper and write a brief list of desires that you have for your life - relationships, career, finances, health etc.

Start with something small from one of those headings.

Develop it into a succinct affirmation that is in the 'as if it has already happened' mode.

(Remember the three 'P's, Positive, Present tense and Personal).

Raphael will help you with clarity, so ask him how you should word it for the utmost effect. He will help with joy, fun and laughter. He is all about the air element, and so he enjoys expressions of happiness and laughter.

Surround the list now with his emerald green light, and ask him to take it out to the cosmos.

This is just your 'starter for ten', as you become adept at this, you can try larger projects. Don't forget to thank him for his assistance and tell him you will see him next time.

Depart with love and lightness and come back to the room and open your eyes. Hello wonderful world!

Archangel Uriel

The Angel of power and peace whose name means 'Fire of God' he brings us peace, wisdom, serenity and self-empowerment into our lives. He is the peacemaker, looking for the peaceful solutions for individuals and nations around the world. He promotes our oneness, our sisterhood and brotherhood, looking for the common ground for peaceful settlements of conflicts.

Archangel Uriel frees you from the bondage of fear, builds your self-belief and self-esteem, raising your confidence and courage to high levels. He is responsible for the third chakra - the solar plexus, promoting willpower to harmonise with everyone and everything.

The colour associated with him is a rich ruby red and he is in charge of the sixth ray, known as the ruby ray of devotion and idealism. I feel particularly motivated by, and connected to Uriel, because I am aware that part of my mission is to bring forward and herald the return of the Divine Feminine, by facilitating the re-empowerment of women and the feminine energy, love, wisdom and compassion in men. Working with Uriel ensures that you will connect to your embedded ancient wisdom and have the confidence to bring it through, and once again I say – "put it out there".

To invoke his power and presence, say the following invocation:

"I invoke the power and presence of the mighty Archangel Uriel to be with me, to bring the strength and courage I require to self-empower, to speak my Truth from the heart with unconditional Love and acceptance. Be with me now, guide me to the deepest parts of my inner sanctum, where my ancient wisdom and knowledge reside. Help me to tap into it now, and bring it forward for the highest good of humanity. And so it is."

Visualisation. (CD Track 1)

Take sacred space, allow about 20 minutes for this meditation.

Close your eyes and take your awareness to your breathing.

Put your roots down into Mother Earth and then connect your crown through a pipeline of Light to the Source of All that is.

Bring yourself into core alignment with Earth and the Universe. Breathe slowly and deeply.

Returning to a gentle in and out relaxed breath simply take your awareness into your Heart centre and enter into its vast space which is like a cave. Go to the end of the cave and you will se a beautiful ruby red glow of light beckoning you forward and down a staircase, leading to a beautiful room, where you will find your Guardian angels, spirit guides and Archangel Uriel's angels.

The glow of ruby red gets stronger as a magnificent tall handsome Angel enters,

Uriel is now with you, offering you a beautiful globe of pure sunlight to place into your solar plexus.

When you do this, you can feel the strength of the sun's rays expanding and radiating throughout your third chakra.

Your breathing deepens to take this amazing Light to all parts of your body now, as you fill up with the direct Love of God and Goddess.

Breathe deeply, expand your lungs with Love.

Archangel Uriel takes you by the hand and leads you into another room which is clearly marked 'Your Future History'.

He asks you to sit down and view a big screen that he is bringing in.

He gives you the controls and the permission to choose what you create on this film of your future.

You enjoy creating, being the film director of your own movie. You include every detail about your future life, how it will be, who the players and stars will be. Your career and relationships will be as you would have them for your highest good.

You enjoy this process, what joy, fun and lightness.

You are the creator, and as you complete the movie, you save it on to a DVD, which you will take with you.

Archangel Uriel is blessing it, dowsing it in his red ruby ray and simply saying to you,

"We bless this creation, if it is for your Highest good and the Highest good of all concerned, so it will be."

Now repeat

"I decree that this creative vision of my future, being for my highest good and the highest good of all concerned, is set in motion and now is, in Divine Right Timing." Say this three times.

Archangel Uriel seals the DVD in a time capsule and fires it off into a waiting and receptive Universe.

Thank Archangel Uriel, as he and his cohorts leave you with your guides, who are celebrating.
Join in the celebration with them, laughing, dancing and singing.

You can revisit this scenario, amend and adjust the movie, and plan as you feel necessary. Always remember to say that the new plan supersedes any declarations made previously.

You return to focus on your heart and your breathing.

Bring your awareness back to the room in your own time with love and joy.

Attunements

This seems an appropriate place to say that during the VIVA workshops, I attune participants to the Archangelic Energy. At Level 1, I attune to Archangels Michael and Gabriel. At Level 2, I attune them to Raphael and Uriel, and at Master Teacher Level, to The Source of All That Is.

Archangel Michael conducts this protocol working through me, it is an intense, life changing experience for all - including me.

Having launched the workshops with VIVA Level1 early in 2007, I have at this time of writing, conducted four of them. I can report that the level of detoxification after the day was extremely powerful, with people presenting with chest and sinus infections, diarrhoea and various other detox mechanisms. They all got rid of a lot of 'stuff' - quite literally.

As a significant number of them were Reiki Masters, it is interesting to note, that even after all the work they have done on themselves, there was still such an enormous shift to be made. This, of course, has strengthened them greatly for future work. It will have raised their vibrational calibration significantly too.

I do not attune you through the energy of this book. Although I know that reading this book and doing the exercises contained in it, will raise your vibration significantly.

I realise that Reiki attunements are available over the world-wide web. I don't dispute that this is entirely possible. I simply don't choose to do it.

When I attune anyone to VIVA, I feel participants need support and guidance throughout the process, and afterwards, during the period of vibration and energy integration.

I don't feel that anything can replace or replicate the wonderful feeling of love and support that comes form a group of like minded folks, meeting in the name of The All that Is, and the Hierarchy of Heaven. It becomes a circle of Love and Light, where sharing, caring, nourishing, safety and security are present.

Archangel Metatron

The mighty Archangel Metatron has been coming in more and more to help me prepare and refine my four-body system for the 5th dimension. He is accredited for having created the electron and is known as 'the voice of God'.

This re-calibration affects the whole structure of our bodies, and as such, Metatron is working on the 7th ray and preparing humanity for the 8th ray.

This is being done with downloads of Light Words, which some are able to repeat as they are given. Judi Satori of the Satori Empowerment Foundation being one such amazing soul. However, we are all downloading information all of the time, and when we choose to get out of our own way and speak what is being given to us to say, we self-empower, and empower the Word of the Source of All That Is.

In the beginning we were created by the Word, and now we are being re-created by the Word, with the sound of the Universe from the depths of Creation.

Metatron is appealing to humanity at this time to release the Vow of Poverty, which you may have taken in a past life, as an expression of your spirituality, to disavow all desire for material things.

This simply no longer serves you or humanity at large. Although the vow was probably taken to expand your wish to spiritually 'serve', there is nothing virtuous about poverty in and of itself.

Metatron is inviting you now to meditate with him and release this dis-empowering bond.

Meditation

Take sacred space,

Take awareness to your breathing.

Bring your body into alignment with Mother Earth, and our magnificent Universe.

Breathe in relaxation and breathe out peace.

As you allow yourself to become more and more relaxed.

When you feel relaxed and deeply connected to your inner being, take your awareness to your Heart centre.

Unlock the secret chamber of your heart, and enter in, acknowledging the tri-fold flame of Spirit within you.

Go to the back of the chamber, and descend the steps there.

When you reach the lower landing, you are joined by the Archangels of Love and Light.

Metatron takes you by the hand and leads you into your inner sanctum.

He is asking you to stand before him.
Put your dominant hand upon your heart, and from the depths of your soul and your being, repeat the following words after him,

'I now choose to release the vows of poverty that I have taken at any time, in any lifetime on any dimension or space.

I cut all ties and connections to these vows,

I do this with the greatest of love and joy. (Breathe)

I see the ties and connectors being removed from my being - now - by the Archangel Michael who is taking all to the Light for Transmutation.

I now align and merge with the energies of Divine Abundance and Divine Blessing in my embodied life.

It is my God given right. And so it is.'

Metatron invites you now to thank all the Archangels and Angels in attendance, and you do so, also thanking him and Mother/Father God.

You are guided back to the stairs where you come back up to your heart centre.

Walk out through your flame - and out of your secret heart chamber, which you lock securely behind you.

When you are ready bring yourself back to the room. Be gentle, loving and kind to yourself.

Take your journal and pen and write down how you felt about this experience.

Archangels and Angels are here, from the other dimensions, to help us. However, we are also blessed with the presence of Earth Archangels and Angels, and I am delighted to say that I regard them to be my wonderful mentors and friends.

Miraculous Mentors

As I write, I am sitting in my office, surrounded by a library of books containing the inspirational words and messages from individuals who have impacted my life significantly.

Dr. Wayne Dyer; Louise L Hay; Maureen Moss; Patti Cota-Robles; Dr. Deepak Chopra; Dr. Doreen Virtue; Patricia Crane; Diana Cooper; Dr. David Hawkins and too many more to mention.

These wonderful human beings have each found their Divine Mission - thank goodness, and have been helping humanity for many years. I feel blessed to have found their work, to have taken on that which resonates for me, its richness, its wealth of wisdom and inspiration. It has helped me through times when I needed guidance, reassurance and a helping hand.

As always, when I, the student, was ready, the teacher appeared. Sometimes a simple validation that what I was feeling was OK was all that was needed. Just to be reassured that I was not losing the plot. The building up of my self–esteem has been my journey this lifetime, remembering who I am, the challenge.

These amazing individuals share their channelled information with great clarity and integrity. I thank them all deeply, and send them great love, because I sometimes wonder if they have any idea of just how deeply profound the work they are doing is, and the impact it is having on humanity's ascension plan at this time.

As they have self-empowered, they have helped you and I to self-empower, and many more voices are now standing up to be heard and be counted.
It won't be long before the critical mass of positive Spiritual energy helps us all rise up to the new 5th Dimension.

As a devotee of Louise L Hay, I have decided to punctuate my book with wonderful affirmations, I first learned to do this years ago on my Louise L Hay training course, and what an invaluable lesson this has been. I use them all the time, because as I have already said, I have no doubt that we were created by the Word, and we are embarked on recreating ourselves with the Word. The power of words and the voice will be discussed in depth later in the book.

I keep them short and simple. First up

Affirmation

"Thank you for the joy"

Say this all day - everyday, I have a wonderful friend who introduced me to this one, and I share it with you with pleasure.

Unconditional Love

Then there is unconditional love. What would a book like this be without this special ingredient, which I have re-grown within my heart? Like my favourite plants, I continue to feed and nourish it within me, so that it is becoming stronger and healthier every day. I bring it to every aspect of my life experience, most recently to my cooking, which is blossoming in every respect.

Isn't love wonderful? Don't you just love to love, love yourself, love everyone, everything, accepting, forgiving, blessing, listening, sharing, giving, receiving, caring with compassion and the deep compassion and understanding of all the Mary's.

Maureen Moss, who has been one of my personal coaches, on and off, for a couple of years, has written the wonderful book 'Commitment to Love'. Every word is meaningful, and worth absorbing at the deepest level. Committing to something, anything, for some people, is difficult, because of their past experiences of getting their fingers burned - always being let down.

When you decide to identify the 'stuff' that is holding you back and dealing with it, (and heaven knows this world is now blessed with many wonderful competent therapists), you can choose to move on, and dare to love.

Nothing ventured, nothing gained, nothing changed, all remains the same.

Choose risk, choose commitment, and choose LOVE.

Archangel Michael also asked me to fall in love with the process of writing this book, rather than regarding it as a chore. I am surprised at the ease with which it is taking shape, and yes, I am adopting a Light attitude to it. He had probably noticed me doing my procrastination thing!

However, now I am in love! I love writing VIVA VOCE, and I know that love will permeate the content in every way.

One last loving affirmation in this chapter before moving on:-

Affirmation

"Thank you for the presence of ever growing Love in every aspect of my life."

Learning and experiences

Just take a few moments to jot down anything you read in this chapter that you found of interest. If you have done the visualisations and meditations, what insights came to you during these experiences and indeed what insights have popped up so far on this book journey?

"Humankind has not woven the web of life
We are but one thread within it
Whatever we do to the web
We do to ourselves
All things are bound together
All things connect."

Chief Seattle
Native American Indian Chief

Energy

We are all one. There is only ever one person in the room. When I heal another or heal myself, I also heal everybody else. I raise the collective vibration. When I abuse another or myself, either verbally, physically or mentally, I am abusing the whole, and I lower the vibrational level of all. Whatever others are doing also affects you and me.

For humanity to heal and find true peace, within and without, we need to choose to focus on the positives in life. Learn to truly love, respect and honour ourselves, others, the planet and accept our Oneness with the All that Is.

To get anything out of this book, there needs to be an understanding and acceptance that everything in and around us is composed of energy vibrating at different frequencies.

Vibration

Energy is invisible, and yet it manifests in form as it vibrates. It all vibrates as sound. Everything on this planet, including the planet, is made of energy. You, me, every thought we have, every word we speak, every bit of food we consume, every magazine we read, every television we switch on, every phone we answer, every virus we have ever had, every illness, every disease. Even time itself is energy.

Energy vibrating is the essence of everything, every creature, every person, every emotion, every animal, every plant and object. You and I, are an electro-magnetic field of conscious energy, sounding, swirling and dancing with grace upon this planet.

Calibration

The only differentiation of how the energy forms shows up, whether it is a person or a table, is the level at which the energy vibrates - which creates a frequency. Scientists measure this by counting the number of cycles per second the energy is moving at. This is called calibration.

For example, a wooden table appears solid, as it is dense and solid. Hence, it is low on the vibration scale. On the other hand, an amazingly loving and light being like Mother Theresa would calibrate high on the scale, as she emanated a lot of light. Her molecular structure was almost totally pure love, and clear of all darkness, shadows or lower vibrational emotional blocks.

Emotions like fear, anger and rage, all have lower vibrations, whereas love, honour and respect, calibrate high on the scale.

Each organ in our body having been through its own individual life experience, also has a vibration calibration and energy print all of its own, showing up at different levels on the scale, depending on each organ's health and well being.

Which scale is that? I hear you ask. Well quite simply, Dr David Hawkins in his book '**Power Vs Force'**, used a scale of 1 to a 1000.

He measured by muscle testing - Kinesiology, the various calibration levels of different individuals and emotional states and illnesses - amongst many other things. The results were intriguing. You really need to read his book in its entirety, if you haven't already done so.

Dr Hawkins states that the words that Christ spoke during his sermons were at the top of the shop - 1000. They were the TRUTH. He did point out that over the centuries, various religions, Popes and Kings have adjusted and altered the Bible to suit their needs. Apparently, the effect of this has reduced the calibration level to 400.

Back to the test. I decided to measure levels of calibration myself along with some colleagues and friends. The average of the results are as follow:

Usui Reiki Energy	801
Karuna Reiki Energy	842
Seichem Reiki	850
Archangelic Energy	1000 and off the scale
Mother Father God Energy	1000 and off the scale
Christ Consciousness Energy	1000 and off the scale

I have to confess the 'off the scale' bit intrigues me, as I had set the 1 to 1000 level before starting. It felt to me as if the Archangels and the Hierarchy of Heaven will simply not be contained in such a scale!

These are interesting results. As a Usui Reiki Master, I would have thought that the original Reiki would have been the purest, therefore calibrating at a higher vibration than its newer cousins, Karuna and Seichem. Well, that's my logical left brain for you.

It is wonderful to know that the Archangels, who are guiding this book and my work, are as high a vibration as 1000+. It explains why people working with the energy on the workshops are experiencing high detoxification levels. We ask these Illumined Beings to be gentle and patient with us as we change the body on all four levels.

Our Cellular Structure

Let us not forget the make up of our physical bodies and its cellular structure.

Within each cell of our body there is an entire Universe and there are millions of cells in our bodies.

"The human body has 100 million cells, each performing millions of tasks each second. For the body to be healthy and fit, these cells have to function as a resonant, harmonious whole". - Deepak Chopra

Each of these cells has a life of its own, with its own memory from this life and past lives, and they just love to hang on to the good emotional 'stuff' - **and** the not so good 'stuff'.

When we decide to clean up our cellular act and consciously bring our cells into harmony, by raising our vibrations and getting rid of the lower vibrational stuff, we, as the conductor of our own orchestra, begin to orchestrate a healthy, happy and whole life for ourselves.

The good news is - as Time is also energy, we can, of course, do our Cosmic Ordering for the future. Equally, we can do our Cosmic Healing of the past, by altering the cellular structure and our DNA from our past lives, and those of our ancestors. At the same time, having a very positive effect on the generations of the future. What we are doing now will affect the next seven generations.

Sub Atomic Particles

The quantum physicists talk about protons, neutrons and quarks being at the very centre of our subatomic particle life, our whirling pool of energy. A quark is infinitesimal, and is pure light. So, we are made of pure light.

DNA recipe

Added to this cellular structure is a matrix called DNA, which holds the formulae that constructs us. It, in the case of human beings, holds the historical and ancestral data, the configuration of your shape and height, and all the genetic information necessary to grow a functional human being.

I am always fascinated by potatoes. Even if you leave them in a dark cupboard and forget all about them, they will still grow their shoots and roots and fulfil their programme, as decreed by their configuration. They still achieve their purpose.

Source

We all come from the same Source of energy. When we understand that we are all connected to each other, there is no such thing as separation. We are all brothers and sisters under the same sun, breathing the same air. We are all part of one great Source of energy.

Our Aura or energy field emanates out from our physical body. We have our four-body system. The field is expansive, and it merges with all the other fields out there. We are one with the collective consciousness, collective intelligence and collective ignorance - whether we like it, or not.

We are not separate from anything or anybody. Therefore, we are collectively responsible for everything that goes on, on this planet. So many of us experience inner conflict within ourselves. The critical mass of stress and inner conflict reflects on our outer experience as war and disquiet, in various places around the world.

If we agree that we can only ever change ourselves, and not control and manipulate others, then we are acknowledging that by finding inner peace, peace will manifest all over the earth.

We are all one, that includes the despotic leaders, the terrorists, drug dealers. Then there are the murderers, the paedophiles, thieves, religious zealots and abusers of varying degrees. That describes the lower vibrational field. The darkness as some would say. Where there is darkness there is (thank goodness) always the Light.

We are also one with wonderful spiritual beings who are on this planet at the moment. People of great spirituality, integrity, honesty, generosity of spirit and unconditional love. And there are many around.

Most importantly, we are one with the Source of All that is. The energy that created all of this Universe, and millions of others. We are at one with, and have Christ consciousness within each and every cell of our body. We are at one with Mother/Father God. This is not a vague concept of something 'out there' that we have to please or humour, or we will be 'cast down'. It is an inner experience, without doubt, the greatest free gift you have ever received and you have it - because you exist!

We are all a combination of Light and Dark. When we focus on expanding the Light within ourselves, it will expand. When we intend to acknowledge, name and deal with the darkness inside, we are able to transmute it to the Light. It will go to the Light.

As this realisation sinks in, we begin to remember that we are all one. Not separate at all. Part of the amazing tapestry and web of life, each being our own little part of the Universal jigsaw - totally unique.

Each one of us matters, because when we begin to vibrate at our full potential level, we become strong and able to support the jigsaw pieces on either side of us, completing the picture.

We started with religions, organised worship of Gods that are 'out there' somewhere. We moved from that to 'a spiritual life', where we took control and connected to God or Spirit, and managed that on our own. However, I know that the new paradigm we are being called upon to seed at this time in humanity's ascension process, is the understanding of 'ONENESS'.

Acknowledging that All is part of you, and you are part of the All, and that includes whatever you perceive the highest vibration of 'All' that there can be as well. There is simply no separation, except that which we choose to introduce ourselves through judgement and fear.

Judgement and fear - they are what cause the blocks in our electro-magnetic energy field, and bring blocks in to the flow of our life.

As well as fear and judgement, blockages occur when we allow our emotional baggage to back up. It is like the drains in the house getting choked with debris. When we don't release it, it is held in the cellular structure of our body, and can cause disease, discomfort, anxieties, phobias, irrational fears and addictions.

These blocks exist from this lifetime, and from past lives as well. As we peel away the layers of the onion that we wear like an overcoat, we really find ourselves on an adventure of self-discovery or re-discovery, as we remember who we are.

I am not a scientist. I am a Lightworker, a Loveworker and Mystic. I have come to the knowledge that everything is energy vibrating through the path of the mystic. It is wonderful that modern science is proving and validating what the mystics have been saying for centuries.

Choosing to Recalibrate

Now that you have an understanding of all that, how can we use this knowledge?

When we begin to understand our energetic make up, the fact that it is vibrating sound, and that our cellular structure and memory is holding on to all the old 'Stuff', we can use this information consciously to improve the quality of our lives by:

- choosing to let go
- surrendering the old baggage
- clearing our drains and chakras
- raising our vibration
- and empowering ourselves to ascension.

In short, choosing to recalibrate.

There are many people who are consciously working to clear the emotional baggage from their lives. Constantly lifting, sifting and shifting their vibrations to new heights. As we are all ONE, this affects the whole, and when we reach a critical mass of more and more people adopting a positively aware and spiritual life, a major shift in vibration will take place for us all.

This is already in motion. Also, Mother Earth is on her Ascension programme. Therefore, humanity doesn't really have a choice. We either ascend with her or flounder on the rocks. As we move towards the 5th Dimension, we must prepare our four-body cellular structure to cope and protect our bodies against increased radiation.

At the risk of being boringly pedantic, I hope you now have a grasp of energy. That it is everything, every being on the planet, from the fish in the sea to the astronaut in the spaceship. Every bug, virus, illness. Every word, thought, feeling, emotion, sound, hiccup, food, furniture - everything!
We are all one, part of the same energy and separate from nothing, including whatever you perceive to be Mother / Father God. That Source energy is in, of, and through us - we are it!

We are ONENESS.

Now, perhaps you already knew this or perhaps it is a bit of exciting powerful news.

Conscious Uses and Application of Source Energy

Wonderful ways of learning about energy, and how to use it consciously abound, such as Spiritual Healing and Reiki Healing. There are now over 30 different forms of Reiki. In these healing modalities, energy is channelled for healing purposes. There are many other ports of call in between with an amazing number of energy therapies now available. The fact is, it is all the same energy (albeit with different levels of calibration) being channelled to heal for the highest good of all concerned.

Having been a Reiki Master Teacher for 10 years, I am well versed in Reiki, and have observed the changes in myself and in those that practice it, offer it and share it. It changes lives significantly, bringing people from almost sleepwalking, through life to awareness and conscious living.

Oneness

As a result of working with the powerful Archangelic energy and VIVA, my psychic channels have opened more and more, and I am now very much aware of when I am being spoken, sounded or sung. However, as I immerse myself deeper in to the ONENESS paradigm, merging with all of the energies, I realise that all of the time, the ALL is working through me. So, when I get angry or raise my voice, that is also part of the All, and the lesson is to accept it the way it is, and not judge it to be good or bad. It just IS.

Acceptance and detachment

A friend and I used to go for long walks around Brodie Castle in Morayshire, and we always ended up laughing because our conversations always came to the same conclusion and with the same saying.

"That's the way it is".

We would end up at acceptance, no matter what challenges we had been discussing. A place of non-judgement, which brought detachment flooding in, this is so freeing.

Practice saying *"That's the way it is"* the next time a challenging situation enters into your life, and notice how it releases you from the drama. Who wants to do drama unless you are addicted to it?

The Introduction of VIVA as an Energy Sound Healing Tool.

The Archangelic realms, principally Archangels Michael and Gabriel, introduced me to a new way of bringing sound vibration into the healing work I do.
Karuna Reiki had introduced me to using sounds to convey symbols as did the KOTADAMA which come in with the Japanese practices of Usui Reiki.

However, I was being asked to do something different, yet incredibly simple, to make intuitive sound healing accessible to all.

I was being asked to re-empower the Divine Feminine in men and women and balance it with the Divine Masculine. To help them find their voices and begin to use them in the easiest of ways - to bring peace and harmony into their lives.

This would have the knock on effects of increasing self-love, self-respect, self-honour, self-worth and self-esteem in all its guises. It would facilitate the release of judgement and fear, moving them into a space of self-forgiveness and self-acceptance.

Finding their own voice and its full potential as a healing instrument, helping them to find the life that really resonates with their own vibration and not dancing to someone else's tune.

The sound would be divinely guided and would be totally unique at every stage. Simple exercises would come through to help people find their Heart voice and Heartsound.

My affirmation became

"I am an inspirational instrument of Thy Divine voice, USE ME."

When you start to use this affirmation, Divine Intelligence is listening and it will respond, so be prepared.

Recap

To recap this chapter, you have learned about energy, vibration, frequency and re-calibration. You have been made aware of Energy healing and Reiki.

You have learned that if you choose with conscious awareness to let go of your past traumas, judgement and fear, the Archangels will work with you and through you, releasing and healing your emotional negatives, raising the level of your vibration and accelerating your ascension.

How are we going to do that? In this book we are going to use VIVA, voice and vibration work. The next chapter is your guide to your re-calibration.

'Your voice is there, it is free and it is the most powerful healing tool you possess and, when heard on its own, is always in tune.'

Patricia Iris

The Voice

We each have a unique, beautiful and mellifluous voice. A sound that emanates from us when we open our mouths and the air flows out from the voice box, playing the vocal chords in a similar fashion to that of a woodwind instrument - blowing air into and over the reed.

When used fully, your voice expresses the full spectrum of colour, from dark brown through to pale blue. I'm sure you know someone with - what you would call - a rich deep dark brown voice.

The thing is that so many people just don't use their voice wholly. They only bring a small percentage of themselves to the party. A 100% party attendee would be the actor Brian Blessed, a fine exponent of the dark brown voice, and the comedian, Joe Pasquale, possibly using about 20%.

Now, I am not suggesting that we all become Brian Blesseds overnight. However, there is most likely room for improvement or you wouldn't have lifted this book to read in the first place.

Are you showing up in your life 100%? Are you hiding your Light and true potential from yourself and the world?

The thing is, I believe the voice is an accurate reflection of many things on many different levels. For example, if you are a confident, articulate, knowledgeable person with little emotional baggage, then you are almost certainly a well modulated confident speaker.

If, however, you are or have been in any way suppressed, repressed, oppressed or depressed, then the likelihood is that your voice reflects that by being quiet, slurring and / or punctuated by the desire to constantly clear your throat. It may feel tight, or feel that you have a lump in it.

Sore throats abound, particularly if you are asked to perform or talk at something, or go to a party or gathering where you don't know anyone. You probably breathe in a shallow way, from the upper chest, and speak from there too. There may be a tendency for panic attacks and asthma, as the fear of actually living your life terrifies you.

Let us look at some really simple ways of healing these ways of being, situations and experiences.

'With Angel's breath
I bring you peace and love
With Angel's breath
I bring you love and light'

Patricia Iris

Breathing

Before I even begin to discuss the use of the voice, let's talk a bit about breathing. I think we would all agree that it is essential. If we don't do it, we cease to exist on this physical dimension. What we are not all aware of is, how we breathe, can seriously affect the well being of our four-body system.

I ask students to think of themselves like a beautiful cello. We are all familiar with the shape of a cello, and the base or belly of it is beautifully rounded, and it is there that the rich round tones are made and resonate.

Visualisation

I would like you to close your eyes just for a moment.

- Think of your body as a cello.
- See the cello shape clearly in your mind's eye

- Breathe in and out of that rounded belly, breathing right down to the pubic bone, or the bridge of the cello and out again.
- Do this several times.

Opening your eyes, ask yourself, how did that feel? Do I feel expanded, light headed?

Notice how it feels to really breathe in to your entire being and oxygenate the blood. Breathing in oxygen, the abundance of life itself.

(Head between the knees please, if you have become a little light headed.)

This activity doesn't involve your shoulders at all, so take them out of the picture. They simply shouldn't be moving as you breathe. Learn to use your total lung capacity.

What you don't use simply fades away, so make sure that you are using your lungs and expanding into life as you get older, rather than contracting, bending over and becoming round shouldered with your chest collapsing.

Be a cello.

Affirmations

'I delight in breathing in fully, expanding and filling my lungs with beautiful air and powerful energy'

'I breathe in joy and expand my lungs with love'

The Power of the Voice

"Tell me who you are with the beautiful vibration of your voice. Introduce me to your soul through the sound of your voice."

Patricia Iris

We use our voice in so many different ways. We use it to speak, to sound, to sing, to hum, chant or tone.

The quality of your voice embodies your transmission. It is what you are putting out to your partners, friends and family and the Universe in general. Using breathing techniques and learning how to deeply relax the throat, and producing simple healing sounds, will go a long way to enhancing your current transmission and begin to heal your past, present and future.

Your transmission contains your light quotient, emotional quotient, intelligence quotient, soul knowledge, inner knowings, inner power, beliefs, all societal and ancestral programming and conditioning and all karmic soul patterning.

Let's take time now to access the Heartvoice, the authentic voice of Truth you brought to this lifetime.

This is the voice I encourage you to use from now on. Your authentic voice, one that is really connected to your centre of Love and yet grounded at the same time. I invite you to learn how to speak and sound from the heart.

HEARTVOICE.

Take sacred space, make sure you won't be disturbed for about 20 minutes, and perhaps you would like to be out-with the hearing of anyone in your environment to avoid inhibition or self-consciousness.

I remember when I first started to do this, years ago, I would get uncontrollable fits of the giggles. Energy moves in mysterious ways and it did with me, and yet, as I write that, I also know that it was energy shifting, and laughter is one of the best medicines, it heals.

Meditation (CD Track 2)

- Take your awareness once again to your cello body
- Become aware of your breath and take the breath down to the base of the cello.
- Take four deep breaths in and out. (If at any time, you become a bit light headed, simply put your head between your knees for a few minutes.)
- Now allow your breathing to return to normal, gentle breaths in and out.
- Close your eyes and take your awareness to the final frontier, the inner space inside you.
- Take your awareness to your voice box.
- Notice what it looks like, or if you can't see an image what does it feel or sound like.
- Using your imagination, make a link between your voice box and the base of your spine, mine looks like a piece of flexible spaghetti, but yours may be a beautiful ribbon or an elastic band, whatever you see, it is the right thing for you!
- Now, simply make it stronger and stronger by adding more threads, ribbons, bands or spaghetti. This connection is now very strong indeed.
- Take a deep breath to celebrate that fact.
- Allow your connection to call into and connect with your heart, so that you have created a three way connector. Voice - to base of spine - to your heart.
- Breathe into it and see all the strands becoming stronger and stronger or simply feel or know that it is happening. Have patience, trust and faith.
- Take a deep breath, open your mouth by simply allowing the jaw to drop and make the sound of 'AAhhh'.
- Allow this sound come forth with effortless perfection.
- Keep practising and observe how this voice, coming from your Heart in a grounded way, makes such a beautiful Heartsound.
- When you feel you have achieved this then gently and slowly open your eyes, come back to the room

Write down how you felt about and enjoyed that experience.

Heartsound

The sound of Ah is the sound of the Heart, the Universe, Mother Earth, the Archangelic Realms, The Spiritual Hierarchy, the Source of All that is and is wholly complete in its simplicity. It is a sound that is included in the names of many of the highest vibrational beings such as Buddha, Rah, Yahweh and the list goes on...

Dr Wayne Dyer brought this to our attention when he shared the wonderful Japa meditation with us a few years ago.

The Archangels are asking that you regard 'Ah', to be an essential building block to this work. Always taking the time to anchor your sound as described above to the heart, voice and base. They ask you to practice it often as part of your daily discipline.

Using it will bring the millions of cells in your body from discord to harmony. The more you do this, the more you will begin to notice a beautiful layer of sound underneath the sound that you are making with your own voice. Listen to it, tune in to it. It is velvety, warm, strong, calming and consistent. This is the connection to the Universal Energy and the Source of All that is, entering into your world, bringing with it, peace and calm. As Within, So Without.

Empty Vessel

When you begin to be more aware of the voice that is sounding through you, you can learn how to get out of your own way. By that I mean, relinquishing control of the voice. It is a metaphor for letting go and letting God. Simply allow the sound of Mother/Father God to flow through you. You become an empty vessel, a conductor and instrument if you like, to receive and transmit this sound.

As you do this, the Spiritual Hierarchy will send waves of amazing new high frequency energy through you, which will help heal yourself and others. You will become a catalyst for change as your presence in and of itself is healing.

Male / Female Balance.

Whether you are a man or a woman is of no consequence when you use these exercises, and learn to use your voice wholly. By gradually allowing your voice to go lower and lower, we ladies can develop luscious rich deep voices even although if, like me, you are a top soprano capable of reaching Top C.

Embracing the lower tones, brings with it positive qualities such as a real feeling of get up and go, motivation, determination and strength. It increases the column of the voice, so that you can learn to go up and down it, almost like you run your thoughts up and down the vertebrae in your spine.

The gentlemen embrace the feminine as they allow their voices to go as high as they can go, without tensing the throat and forcing the sound out. This assists them to bring in qualities of compassion and understanding. All of the above assist with balancing the male and female qualities in the four-body system.

Discipline

Working with the sound of Ah will bring more of you to the party of life as healing occurs. The structure of your DNA will be restored stand by strand. This is a gradual process that takes time. So healing with the voice isn't a quick fix, its not just about reading a book and knowing or feeling that the information resonates for you. It is about the daily practice of making the sound of Ah. Perhaps you could do it at the

beginning or end of your normal meditation practice. Whatever time you pick, it really needs to be done daily in order to have the maximum impact.
In later chapters, we will develop the use of this soundisation, and use it in different ways to assist with the healing of many different aspects of who we are, and how we are going to grow ourselves daily. When we bring the power of focussed intention into the formula, we really begin to do amazing work.

Let's have a look now at the speaking voice. In many ways, just as important as the tones sound.

The Spoken Word

When you use your voice to speak, you have choices. You can use it quietly and peacefully, or you can use it loudly and aggressively. You can use it with positive words, constructively or you can use it negatively, destructively.

Positive or Negative.
When you are positive, you build and elevate the vibrations in yourself and others. When you are negative you lower them dramatically.

Have you ever noticed at a meeting, when a particular person arrives they radiate happiness and positivity, and everyone is positively affected by it. Vibration rises and much laughter and lightness follows. On the other hand, haven't we all been to a meeting where an individual arrives who is in a negative, angry space. This energy permeates the atmosphere, and in no time at all, the meeting is flattened, with little inspiration flowing. Basically, it becomes a waste of time.

You have a choice. How are you going to be today from the moment you waken up, and your feet touch the floor?

Daily choices

- To be constructive - or destructive.
- To be positive - or negative.
- To be empowering - or dis-empowering.
- To express the Truth - or not.

Our Truth

Our Truth lives in our third chakra, the gut. My gut speaks loudly to me a lot of the time. If I feel uncomfortable in that area with whatever I am focussing on, or something that is going on in my life, or someone disturbing my inner peace, I need to pay attention and speak up and out. I always tune in to myself to be assured that what I am saying is not coming from a position of unhealthy ego.

So often, we deny our Truth. You will probably have experienced someone, red faced, shouting at the top of their voice, "I am not angry". Clearly not congruent, clearly not the Truth, as blood vessels stick out on their neck and their voice is over loud.
When we express the Truth of our hearts, that is to say, what we truly feel about life or what we need in our lives, we honour ourselves and bring the vibration up. When we don't speak up, when we avoid the Truth and set aside our needs in favour of another, we disrespect ourselves, we let honour fall by the wayside and we betray the beauty and power of our Higher Self and Spirit. We also cause an imbalance.

Universal Laws

The Universe had provided a space for you to speak your Truth, in not doing so, the listener or listeners were denied an opportunity to grow and learn from you . Perhaps it was an opportunity for them to understand you a little more, or hear your amazingly bright idea, or be able to acknowledge with you, your anger or torment. Interestingly, the Universe will keep presenting you with opportunities, until you learn to take them and speak up.

It is also about integrity. Walking your talk, and not going along with things, just to avoid 'rocking the boat'. It is about being your own authority and not giving that away to others.

Interestingly, my husband Bill recently had a lady on his hypnotherapy course who had evidently come on his course, just to get the qualification as she had been practising visualisation and meditation for years although not hypnosis.

She spent most of her time, as he followed the accredited curricula, telling him that,

"this isn't the way I would do this",
"I don't agree with this and that",
"these are baby steps, I know all this".

She talked over and through the training days. Very challenging to Bill, as he tried to keep control of the day and his teaching agenda. When Bill asked her to DO some trance and induction work, she was very inhibited and embarrassed, and didn't really do it very well. The conclusion being that she talked a good talk. However, she couldn't actually come up with the goods. There was no substance or foundation to her work. Her 'act' was really to cover this up. Low self-esteem and low self-worth play out in unusual ways and her domineering bluster was a cover up job. A real test for those interacting with her to find acceptance, understanding and compassion for her.

She simply couldn't be taught anything. She focussed on everything negatively, trying to pull it down. She was a full cup, no room to learn new things, ideas or concepts or to acknowledge that there are always many ways to DO everything.

There are 365 ways of washing the dishes. Openness and flexibility were not part of her personality. It was a case of my way or no way. Whereas Bill chose to exercise all his powers of flexibility, until it reached a point of 'this far and no further'. An interesting journey for both parties.

I am using this as an example of someone who is speaking out and speaking her Truth from a position of low self-esteem. Someone who is not willing to listen to the other person's Truth, and be open to new ways and learn.

Listening is such an important part of communication – often, the most important part. You learn, that in honouring and respecting your own Truth, if it is coming from a position of healthy self-esteem, you will automatically be guided to honour and respect others and their points of view.

Second Guessing

How often do we second-guess how we think someone will react to what we have to say, if we really speak our Truth? We project on to them what we think the reaction will be and that would usually be a negative one.

It took me months to pluck up the courage to speak my Truth to my ex-husband, to tell him that the relationship was dead for me, and that I wanted to move on. I had gone through it so many times in my mind, playing it like a record, extremely fearful of how it would be received. In the event, when I did speak out, we both cried as he knew this was the Truth as well. All of my fears were unfounded, and within a year I was in a completely new life, one which honoured me and my spirit. This doesn't mean to say that it wasn't an emotional and painful time for both of us after 17 years of marriage. However, having aired the Truth, we could deal with it in a mature manner. He quickly found a new and rewarding love in his life and remarried. We could have struggled on, trying to make it work, so as not to upset the children, relatives and the world. It simply doesn't serve to put the rest of the world's wishes before your own.

Voice Power

It is clear we have immense power to build ourselves up or pull ourselves down, simply by the words that come out of our mouths, and we hold that power over others too.

My husband and I went for a walk last evening around beautiful Spring blossoming Blairgowrie. When we started off, I was fresh, however, as we got about a mile or so along the road, I began to feel my legs hurting a little and my lower back making its presence felt. I simply began to say to myself, 'energy, energy, energy down into my legs',

I did this with every step I made until we got home (about 2 miles later). I was striding out and felt really energised by the time we got home. Isn't it a powerful yet simple technique, the power of our own voice and the words we say to ourselves? Why not try it for yourself? You will be amazed.

Misuse of power

Regrettably, there are people out there who misuse this power. Some consciously, others unconsciously. For example, the bully. Whether a child or an adult, the leader of a country or company or business or government, who uses this power to frighten, sometimes terrorise other people, their verbal abuse of others is often accompanied by physical abuse. It is really a projection of their own fear, anger, low self-esteem, self-hatred and inadequacy. They consciously put their venom out there, some of this evil motivated by a greed for money, material goods and power over others.

"When the power of Love
overcomes the love of power,
the world will know peace"

Anon

Unfortunately, the unconscious mis-users of power are quite often dressed in white coats. They have positions of authority, and people follow their words like lemmings over the edge of the cliff.

The saddest part of that kind of negative programming is when someone is told that they only have so much time left to live. They then bring that little prophecy into being by accepting the programme, and obliging, instead perhaps, of allowing God and other forces to, including the body's own desire to heal itself, bring about recovery, miraculously or otherwise. On occasions when these miracles do happen, they are always fobbed off as 'instantaneous remission' with a vague threat of, "it will be back, don't worry".

How positive!

I was somewhat amused last evening, when the BBC announced that a report had been brought out proving that HRT is in fact beneficial to women, and not, as previously stated in the late 1990's, a danger to us all. On the basis of this report, by, well I can't remember now, we are all just supposed to accept that everything is fine after all, and get back into using these chemical drugs. 'THEY' say it is OK.

Hang on, it is now a few days later, and we are back to square one, a new report is out and 'THEY' say, 'it could have been causing Ovarian C'. Just as well we didn't all rush out to get some then!

The Power of Words

'The voice is only as powerful as the words it uses.'

Patricia Iris

There is a great lack of understanding of how powerful words are, particularly in the Health Services. As a fully qualified clinical Hypnotherapist, I have observed over the years that we are really being hypnotised, one way or another - all the time. The hypnotisers in chief being the media, whether they are acting on behalf of a company and advertising their wares, or whether they are acting as the voice piece for the government, constantly going over and over the various news stories that are current. They, as you will undoubtedly have noticed are mostly negative situations. Not ones that we can do a lot about. So, a feeling of helplessness and inadequacy follow on, and guess what, our vibrations go down. Just occasionally something like the London Marathon comes on which lifts our spirits. We decide that there is a little good in the world after all and our vibrations rise.

Constant affirmation of this negative stuff can, and often does affect people in a serious way. They don't understand why they are feeling depressed, that they are developing irrational fears for their safety in the world at this time. The stress of day today living takes its toll, and before long, they are 'off work' with stress related problems.

Why do we watch the news? Why do we buy newspapers that trade in this negative stuff all the time? When will we, as a nation, a race, learn to focus on what we want in our lives and not on what we don't want?
We all have a responsibility to *take responsibility* and speak up and out. Regrettably, in the UK there is a feeling of resignation as to the state of the country. Individuals not standing up and speaking out about how they feel. Hopefully, this book will help you to find the confidence and the self-empowerment to stand up and make a difference. Too long, particularly in Scotland, have we been scared to stick our heads above the parapet for fear of being shot down. The time has come to rid ourselves of the ancestral patterns of subjugation, to anyone or anything. We all count!

If positive affirmations work, so do negative ones. Isn't it about time that, as we learn to stand up and speak out our Truth, that we take control, stop buying the papers and feeding the monsters and watch less, if any news at all. We can make changes when we vote with our buying power and our remote control.

We could also choose to stop being members of www.whingers.com. This is fake web site, at least I think it is, that I made up recently, because a number of people very close to me whom I shall not name to spare their blushes kept going on and on about 'things' that happen. Going on about the government, the systems that rule the country, the war, the this, the that. The effect of this is to constantly reaffirm what we <u>don't</u> want, by energising it with words. There are no 'BUTS' about this. It is about consciously choosing <u>not</u> to give energy to these situations or words. It gives <u>them</u> power.

This does not mean that we go into denial about the atrocities that are committed in the world, to people, men women and children, to animals and to the planet herself. Certainly not! We can only begin with focussing on ourselves, our integrity and our honesty. Clean our own acts up, and use our voices in a powerful and positive way, to lead the way for positive changes on this planet. We need to start now. The time has come when it just isn't good enough to sit back and let it all happen. We need to start manifesting and creating what we want in life.

Take time right now to list what you would like to see in this world, on this planet right now. Come up with seven things that you would create if you had a magic wand to wave over humanity.

1. ....

2. ....

3. ....

4. ....

5. ....

6. ....

7. ....

Well done.

Now build a wonderful story around them. Mine would run something like this.

"In this beautiful world that I live in, peace prevails. There is enough food and water to feed us all and it is well distributed around the world. Wealth is also distributed fairly with companies and businesses recognising, honouring and valuing their employee's contributions to their success. All the animals on this planet are treated with love and respect, and as brothers and sisters who have feelings, and they love us in return. Education and personal development is free for all, children and adults. We specialise in educating them all about Mother Earth and how she needs to be treated to heal her and support her. The health of humanity has been restored to wellbeing, as Energy healing is freely available for all, and instruction on this is available in all our Universities and Colleges. Music and sound in all their guises are brought back into all nurseries, schools and college curricula and humanity are encouraged to sing joyfully together to create renewed harmony, bringing us closer and closer together, remembering their brotherhood and sisterhood. We join together and sing together from the same spiritual hymn sheet, a joyous race At Oneness with the Source. Co-creating with the Source of All that is, humanity creates heaven on earth.

Vibrational life of words

I love lecturing, talking to, sharing with and teaching groups. I love using our rich language to its fullest. I enjoy the words, every syllable, knowing that as I speak, I am altering the vibrational state of all those listening. How do I know this? Because I am acutely aware of the vibrational life of words and their innate ability to heal.

I am also aware of the co-creating energy that works through me, making me the catalyst for change in others, simply by saying something that will trigger a change or release in the listener.

For example: the energy field that is this book. It would be interesting to evaluate the calibration level of its content, because it is pure energy being channelled from the Higher Realms of consciousness. So, even if you don't read it, just by having it in your possession, it will shift your vibrational level. If you enjoy reading at night just before you go to sleep, place it under your pillow. The contents will enter into your consciousness through your vibrational field.

Water

Masaru Emoto in his wonderful books on Water and its magnificent qualities, has validated completely what I have always felt about thoughts, words and language. He carried out tests on water, photographing its cells before, and after having had wonderful positive words spoken to it, or written on the water containers, or even positive thoughts directed at it. The results are stunning.

When water hears or receives the word or thought 'Gratitude', or a similar positive word or thought like 'Peace' for example, its cellular structure forms itself into a beautifully constructed design, like that of a snowflake. When he shows you specimens of water from negative situations prior to the positive words and thoughts, you can see very clearly, how contaminated mis-aligned and out of balance the water has become. It looks distorted and mis-shapen. I urge you to buy his books on the subject, and see this amazing evidence for yourself.

Thoughts

He places most of his emphasis on thoughts, and how they affect the molecular structure of the water. I believe that when we 'name' a thought and put it out there, the power increases 100 fold.

Negative thoughts and fears.

Not to name some thoughts, ones of anger and resentment can cause blockages in your piping as it were. Perhaps, if you are an addict or homosexual, and decide, through fear of familial or societal condemnation, to keep it to yourself or at another level, don't admit it to yourself, remain in denial, this too causes blockages. This can lead to all kinds of mental disturbances and physical dis-eases, with the guilt and shame level high sometimes leading to suicide.

It may not always be appropriate to express your anger or suppressed fear in public. However, there are ways of getting it out of your system that are quite remarkable in their effect.

Exercise.

Create sacred space. Play some gentle music and relax.

Take your journal and pen. List all of the things that you have chosen not to share with the rest of the world, because you feel guilt, shame, fear, anger, resentment and or disillusionment.

Write them down.

Now, we have choices and options. You can:

- Ceremoniously read them out to the Universe and then burn the paper, releasing the energy of emotions to the element of fire and Archangel Michael who will come in as you call him forth to take this energy, transmute it, and bring in Light.

- Find some woods out in the country, obviously a quiet spot where you will not be heard and where you can safely shout out at the top of your voice

"I release this 'Anger' (or whatever it is, complete the whole list) to Father Sky, Mother Earth and the four directions, knowing that it will be transmuted to the Light by the Source of All that Is. I now choose to love and accept myself exactly as I am right now, and I am OK, I am a child of the Universe with every right to be here, I count! And so it is."

- Do this as often as you like, until you feel a shift of vibration.

In your sacred space, make up a chant or song holding the fears and feelings you want to transmute. An example would be:

"I now choose to name my Truth, I................., I am what I am. I now choose to accept myself and forgive myself, if I have done anything to upset others. I am always doing the best I can at any given time. I now choose to love myself as never before. I move forward, make life expanding and enhancing decisions for myself. I am taking control'. Sing out loud, sing out strong.

Choices

These are just possibilities, remember not to put me in a white coat and hang on every word as gospel. At some level, everything in this book is for you to read and take on board, only if it feels right for you. Your heart, not your head, will know the answer to that one.

Detox warning. After this work has been done you could experience an extreme tearful release or it could be sneezing.

It could manifest later with headaches and or diarrhoea. Drink lots of water, about 1.5 litres a day and pop in a slice of lemon to alkalise it.

Follow whichever method you have chosen up with powerful words of affirmation,

I am, I am what I am, and it is OK to be me.

I am learning to deeply and profoundly love and approve of myself.

Every day in every way I choose to be more loving and respectful to myself.

I love, honour and respect who I am.

Names

I have discussed naming emotions and statements of fact, however what about our names? The identification tags we were given as children. Do they reflect who you really are? Are you comfortable with your name?

On my workshops I carry out an exercise that really has profound effects. Just asking everyone to tune with their Heartvoice and Heartsound and state their name out loud a few times, brings the realisation to hand for some - that they really do not resonate with their names.

Surnames

I find this a lot with surnames. Women often hang on to their married name, even though they are divorced, not realising that the energy of that union is being prolonged as long as they use that name. It is a cord or tie just like any other kind. In fact, it is the one that sealed a vow. It needs to be consciously addressed, or at some level, they are still in that old relationship, which presumably, they dissolved as it didn't work or it was toxic.

I know that many people want to keep on good terms, and rightly so, with their ex partners. However, not to let go of the name is not to sever properly from the vows made. It perpetuates the tie, not allowing a new relationship to enter in, or indeed the new relationship they <u>are</u> in, will never truly blossom, as long as one foot is firmly in the past.

I can hear some cries of "I am perfectly happy with that name. I have been using it for years. People know me as that. I have an identity that hinges all around that'.

Absolutely right, it is a label you have worn with comfort, and then discarded the label bearer. I am simply flagging up what is going on at another level. In all honesty, has part of you been hanging on to that ex partner or husband? Only you know the Truth of that but <u>do</u> be honest with yourself.

If you are professionally known by the old name, keep it for that part of your life, if you feel that is a must. However, changing the other is worth consideration. It is like re-creating who you are, withdrawing your power from the 'old' and the 'past' and moving fearlessly into the new you. It may be scary at first, but what a fantastic opportunity!

Didn't Susan Jeffers really crack it when she coined the phrase:-

'Feel the Fear and do it anyway!'

First Names

First names are often the subject of much discomfort with people, who really object to being called by nicknames or shortened versions of their actual name. We teach people how to treat us, and if we allow this level of disrespect to carry on, it will. So there is always an opportunity to respect yourself.

Simply say, "I prefer to be called Patricia" - or whatever your name is.

If you prefer the shortened version, it could be an indication that you are resisting taking on the mantle of the fullness of who you are, just notice this. It is not to be judged or criticised, perhaps this will change sooner than you think.

When I consciously chose not to take on my new husband's name last year, I was guided to really look into the use of my middle name, which is 'Iris'. I looked it up on the web and came across the following information on the Goddess called IRIS. .

- IRIS was the goddess of the rainbow, a messenger of the Olympian gods.
- She was later described as a handmaiden and personal messenger of the goddess Hera.
- Iris was a goddess of both the sea and sky – her father Thaumas "the wondrous" was a sea god, and her mother Elektra "the amber" a shining cloud godddess.
- For the coastal-dwelling Greeks the rainbow's arc was most often seen spanning between cloud and sea.
- Iris had no distinctive mythology of her own. In myth she appears only as an errand-running messenger and was usually described as a virgin goddess.
- Iris was depicted in ancient Greek vase painting as a beautiful young woman with golden wings holding a herald's rod (*kerykeion*), and sometimes a water-pitcher (*oinochoe*), in her hand.
- She was usually shown standing beside Zeus or Hera, often serving nectar from a jug. As nectar-pourer Iris was indistinguishable from Hebe.
- Her name had a clever double meaning, being connected with both *iris*, the rainbow, and *eiris*, a messenger.

Her father was Thaumas and her mother Electra.

This really resonates for me, as I really feel like a messenger being used more and more to deliver the words of the Illumined Beings of Light. I have always been drawn to colours and their therapeutic vibration and value therefore the 'rainbow' aspect is also pertinent. My father was called James Thomas, so there again is a connection with THAUMAS. I believe we do choose our parents.

I also am a great user and lover of Flower essences. I came across a flower essence made by Harebell Flower Essences in Southwest Scotland, and here are the healing properties of that particular remedy.

IRIS (Iris Germanica)

'Empowering.
For coming into ones own personal power. Being our own authority and withdrawing that invested in others.
Releasing blocks to creativity and living to our full potential.'

Well, I couldn't have written the script for my life any more succinctly or accurately. That is what I am all about, to empower myself and give others a hand up to empower themselves.

Your Name

We are truly blessed with an infinite amount of knowledge on the world-wide web, so do get on to your computer and find out as much as you can about your name, its roots and its meaning. If it doesn't resonate with your vibration simply ask the Archangels to bring forward a name to you that really makes your heart sing. Then, notice the signs and what happens.

Messages on the TV, radio, billboards, or someone repeatedly calling you by a different name, are all signs. I have done this in workshops when I have felt that someone is an 'Angela' for example however their name perhaps is 'Ann'. When I have made the error of using the wrong name, I apologise of course. However, they quite often say that that was a dear relative's name, or one they like, or one that people often call them by mistake.

Nothing happens by accident and it is worth noticing all the synchronicities that will come into play when the Universe conspires to find the right name for you!

You will really self-empower when you choose to take the time to change your name if that is what feels right for you. You will then resonate in the fullness of it. Because I have done this a number of times, I will offer you my list of people who have to be notified. In Scotland, you can change your name to be known as something else without referral to the law. I believe the law is different in England, so best check up with that.

The List.

- Passport
- Banks
- Credit Cards
- Utilities
- Driving Licence
- Clubs and Associations
- The Phone book

- Post office
- Registration with any businesses
- Your employer.

You will notice a big difference when you are standing in the power of the name that makes your heart sing.

Self-Talk

Our bodies are at least 85% water, so you don't need to be a scientist to work out that if water reacts to words and thoughts, then we, (who are virtually water) are going to do just the same. Here was I, for many years as a Hypnotherapist and Psychotherapist, thinking it was all down to the power of the sub-conscious mind. And no, I'm not throwing that theory in the bin. The subconscious is the home of all past life memories. However, there is an elegant Universal simplicity in how positive self-talk and positive talk in general works.

By building yourself up with encouragement everyday, there will simply be nothing you cannot achieve. You will be able to achieve all of your goals.

Add this new use of positive words to your new found ability to breathe really deeply, and speak from the cello belly of the body. You will notice how rich and smooth your voice becomes, and how it magnetises different things to you, because you are changing your transmission, consciously and unconsciously, re-calibrating your vibration. The more you practice this, really becoming aware of every word that comes out of your mouth, or that you speak to yourself, the more your life will positively change and the lives of those around you.

Buy some rubber bands immediately folks, and put one on your wrist! Every time you become aware of thinking negatively or speaking negatively, twang your wrist band and you will find that at the end of the day your wrist will be pretty red. We are all a lot more negative than we think we are!

Affirmations

With this new information about water, just think how amazingly powerful affirmations really are. When I first read 'You can Heal Your Life' by Louise L Hay, I busied myself repeating affirmations, doing exercises and making up new ones daily. This to me was/is the most wonderful book I have ever read. I soaked its contents up like a sponge. Pure common sense, and somehow deep down I felt I knew the substance of it, and I was just remembering the information given. I thought that I was reprogramming my subconscious mind. I am sure that is true, as we all have deeply hidden ancestral patterns and karmic soul patterns activating in our lives.

Dumping the old and reprogramming for the new is a must, as we know from earlier chapters. However, what about simply sitting and chanting the word LOVE over and over? Allow it to permeate every cell, every atom, every sub-atomic particle in your body. This energy of course, is manifesting as water, blood, muscle, bone and it is the water content that is the key.

Chanting 'love'

Try it, now. Take 5 minutes to close your eyes, focus on the word LOVE and begin (with the focussed intention of balancing your four-body system) to chant it over and over again. Use whatever note comes out your mouth, and notice the pleasing effects that it has. Notice the sense of well being that is coursing through your body as your body responds to the words, the sound and the focussed intention. Five minutes of this should be enough to make you feel calm, peaceful and loving. If you like, you can visualise all the darkness floating away from you like little worms. Simply ask the Angels of love and light to come and cleanse them all away for you as you do this. They will be transmuted and taken to the Light.

Now we know why the Beatles had such a fabulous hit with their song, 'All you need is Love.'

Focussed Intention

I have, in the last couple of years, really taken on the message about focussed intention, and how it helps us to co-create our reality with the Divine. Everything I do now, I check in to see if it has Divine approval and, if it does, I proceed to give it my all. It is like an archer aiming at the target with his/her bow, fixing my total attention and commitment to hitting the target on the nose - as it were.

I used to be really good at going on diversions. Little trips off on one project or another that took my focus away from my own work, to other people's projects.

I always had a great yen to help everyone on the planet achieve their goals, until one day, I thought, 'Hang on, if I keep doing this, I'm not going to achieve my own goals, so I really must learn to choose my own purpose first, get my message out there and then help others as much as I can, with the remaining energy I have, if it is for my and their Highest good'.

The more I respect myself, and honour my soul purpose, the more other people respect me, and that is always the way, is it not?
As within, so without.

Creating Monsters

We have discussed the vibration and calibration of various things in the Universe. I wonder what you think is the level of calibration for the diseases, Cancer or Aids? The words in themselves can and often do strike fear into the individual, lowering their vibration. The names themselves now hold such a dark force, a dark power that anytime any being on this planet thinks about them, or talks about them, they are energised. Remember, what we focus on expands. Not only that, if we make it the focus of our attention, over and over, just as the positive magnetisation occurs, so too does the negative. We are effectively inviting that energy into our field. We have created giant negative entities.

For wonderful scientific information on this I direct you to a book called, 'It's the Thought that Counts' by my friend Dr David Hamilton. He explains this whole phenomenon with left-brained terminology, yet in a way we can all understand easily.

So, just think of the amazing result that could come from everyone refusing to energise these illnesses any longer, dis-empowering them, not naming them, not focusing on them, not allowing the news on TV and radio to constantly feed the monsters. We could choose to focus on health and promote wellbeing, loving, touching and caring. We would have a society that is more powerful, loving, healthier and taking responsibility for its wellbeing. Remember everything is energy, even these life threatening diseases. We can release and change the energetic blocks that are at the root of these energetic malfunctions in a number of ways to effect healing.

The Inner Critic

We are also adept at taking our energy down. Have you met my friend and yours, your 'Inner Critic'?

What a star he/she is. Your own in-house commentator. Always there to let you know just how it was, and you can bet your life it wasn't good enough!

- "You should have done it this way or that"
- "that was a stupid thing to do"
- "why didn't you say this or that"
- "maybe you need to push here or there to get what you want."

Endless diatribe of criticism flows from his or her lips, I hear about it from participants all the time in workshops, whenever I speak about everyone having a wonderful unique sound to make with their voice.

For example:

Negative message.

"She hasn't heard my voice"

'Inner Critic' at work with self-judgement, comparing with others, not as good as....

"I hate the sound of my own voice, it's too..."

How on earth do we expect to thrive, if we are hating any part of ourselves. Our bodies are magnificent temples that house our spirits, and our soul's communication device, the voice. Our voices, when loved and cared for, will respond amazingly well, like any muscle when used regularly in the proper way, they will become finely tuned. Self-rejection and self-hatred are not vibration lifting sentiments.

Affirmation

"I am beginning to love the sound of my voice more and more."

Negative message

'I was always told to 'shut up' at home so what I have to say must be no good, I don't matter, I don't count'

This is wearing, constantly being told to 'be quiet' or 'shut up' or 'f.... off'. Eventually, it gets through. It's like training a puppy to sit or beg. I learned as a child to be quiet and be invisible. Is this true for you? Learned behaviours like this also lead to self-doubt, low self-worth and low self-esteem, making it more and more difficult as you get older to really stand up and stand out with your Truth.

Become aware of how you speak to your own children. We all have a responsibility with all the awareness of the learning's from our own lives, to bring up children feeling loved, encouraged and listened to.

Humanity's mantra of being so busy, work; work; working, they have little time for appreciating each other.

Mum feels – "here I am, standing at the sink, making meals, clearing up, non stop, nobody notices….."
Dad feels - "here I am, out everyday working my b…. off, providing for everyone, and I don't even get a hug when I come in the door.

Your brothers and sisters feel that they are invisible too, as perhaps you don't really connect much with them either.

Suggestion.

Set aside time for the family at least once a week and yes, have that mutual appreciation society. Why not? You are asked to focus on what is good and wonderful about each other, leave criticism at the door and notice how, as you feed the entity called your family, it grows in love. Remember what you focus your energy on expands in your life, so focus on positivity - and the negativity will simply fade away.

The free spirits that are being born these days, need to be tamed a little, that' s all, not controlled beyond belief, towards suffocation.
I do however, see and hear children being able to speak up and out, and that is truly wonderful, as we have such a lot to learn through the eyes of the children.

Sometimes, as an adult, not being listened to at home or at work is a mirror of how the individual is not listening to the innermost promptings of their heart or in-tuition. When we listen to ourselves, others listen to us too. When we stand in our power and don't 'shut up' as the bully suggests, we shift the vibration. Be Brave, speak your Truth up and out, it really counts.

Affirmation

"I am learning to honour my inner voice and speak up and out fearlessly, what I have to say really counts."

Negative message

"I had to be seen and not heard"

This one causes havoc in later life when you are asked to make reports at management/ business/personal/committee meetings, getting your point across effectively, searching for the gap that sometimes never comes, because you are too reticent to speak up and out.

Affirmation

"My input counts, I have inspirational ideas and comments to make that are welcomed by my colleagues, my voice deserves to be heard".

Negative message

"You are stupid"

This one is alive and well. Children really take it on board, and can begin to behave that way, even if they are not stupid. Monitor your mouth if you are a parent. What comes out of it has lasting effects!

The thoughtless use of this kind of language is more about the adults, lacking in patience and tolerance of the youngsters, (back to the mantras of the busy life). Children are just a bit slower at times at making the connections that we are so used to making. This seems to happen particularly in the teenage years. It can be hormonal, with chemical changes taking place in the body.

Adults, of course, who have had a large dose of this little programme, emerge into work life with an even larger dose of low self-esteem, feeling inadequate and not good enough. They don't feel 'enough', and feel they cannot come up with the goods. Because they believe this to be true, that is what they manifest for themselves. We are co-creating our lives with the Source, with every word we say, with every thought we think and every feeling we feel. We need to change this erroneous belief.

Start now by affirming

Affirmation

"I am good enough. Everyday, in every way, I am getting more and more empowered, to be who I really am. I love and approve of myself."

This 'not good enough' message plays out in your inner playground anytime you are asked to deliver a report, or present something to a number of people. You would rather die than stand up and speak out. Apparently, public speaking is one of the greatest and most common fears that individuals hold. This usually means you don't do yourself justice. You suffer from stress, sweating, palpitations, urgent need to go to the loo and / or panic attacks. Does that sound familiar?

The written word

Your voice also goes out through the written word. So, how many of you put pen to paper? Noting down your take on what is going on, writing your music, songs or poetry.

'Don't die with your music still in you.'

Anon

Uniqueness

There are 6.4 billion people on this planet and no one else has your finger print, your eye print, your DNA (Except perhaps an identical twin) or your VOICEPRINT. Your voice is UNIQUE, and as such, has come in with you, to express your unique recipe. The recipe, with all its unique ingredients, that you agreed to deliver to Humanity at this time right now.

I hear clients and students saying,
"Oh, but I don't know what I am here to do, I'm not sure what my purpose is. Perhaps I should go on a workshop to get to the root of that."

The Universe and Source have really tried to keep it simple in so many ways, and here we go complicating things again.

A human being is just that - a spirit within a human body, who is 'being' and 'experiencing'. You don't need to 'BE' any particular thing - except the essence of who you are - which is 'love'. When you allow that to flow, your presence radiates healing, and raises the vibrations of all life you encounter, and affects the area where you live for about a ten mile radius.

A human being is here to serve others with Love. So, how can you serve today? That is the question. When you listen to your heart and the Divine Light within, you will become aware of gentle promptings or inspiration. As long as you listen to the inspirational messages of the heart, you will self-actualise. However, that involves mastering ego, the left brain and the inner critic. Loving them until they have no control over you. When your heart's desire is being fulfilled, you will be, and are serving humanity.

"To stand in the Light is a virtue
To reflect the Light is your path
To Be the Light is all that you are"

Judy Satori

Your Inner World

Let's look at that thought. You are going to love your Inner Critic into bliss and acceptance. Let's empower that thought by speaking it out loud with intention, remembering that when we intend to do something, Divine Intelligence is listening and responding. Suddenly, high powered help will be available to help us achieve our goal.

"**I intend to Love my inner critic into bliss and acceptance. To let it go to the Light with my infinite blessings and gratitude**."

Say this three times with feeling and really mean it.
Make sure the Universe cannot miss this message. Shouting it out in the woods would be ideal. You could also write a letter to your Inner Critic, and then, ceremoniously burn it.

"Thank you so much, dear inner critic. I acknowledge that you came in to my field of consciousness for a purpose. However, the time has come for you to go, as I take back control of my co-creative process with Source, and decide to let go of a constant need to criticise and sabotage my life."

It is also possible that this is a Karmic Soul Pattern of not being 'good enough' that is playing out and through you, and has been doing so for aeons. So, now it is time to let this go and heal it.

With all this focus on the negative Inner Critic, which may have taken your vibration down a bit, the Archangels are prompting me at this time to guide you through a visualisation, vibrationisation and feelingisation. How do you like all the 'isations'? They work! They also drive the spellchecker mad. (Dr David Hamilton coined the feelingisation one first).

The Archangels are going to introduce you to your very own Inner Promotor, Inner Appreciator, Inner Lover, Inner Valuer, Inner Teacher and any other positive' Inners' you can think of, that I can't think of, at this moment. Let's celebrate that we can, and will create our own Inner Experience right now, and watch with joy, as it affects our outer experience, in so many positive and empowering ways.

Take sacred space. Take time to get in to your Sound Dome. When you feel safe and comfortable there, have someone read this to you.

Archangelic Guidance to empower your Inner World.

- Gently close your eyes if they are not already closed.
- Take your awareness to your breathing.
- Notice the beautiful air as it enters into your nostrils. Savour its coolness, and enrich your entire four-body system by breathing really deeply into the depths of your being before exhaling, ridding yourself of any toxins that have accumulated.

Do this three times.

- Returning to normal breath please take your attention to your heart.
- Find the key to the secret chamber of your heart and open the door.
- Walk through, and you will see before you the threefold Divine flame that is your part of the All that is, that resides within you.
- Walk through the flames, feeling the cleansing and cooling touch of this Divine Light as it embraces you.

- As you emerge, you can now see in front of you, a beautiful doorway, that takes you on to a landing with a spiral staircase.
- This takes you down to a lower level within your heart.
- There are ten steps. Descend them, one at a time, taking your time and acknowledge your guardian angel, dearest ones, he/she is beside you supporting you on your journey
- Upon reaching the lower level, you walk along the hallway to a great door.
- This door is opened for you and you walk through into your inner cathedral.
- As you look around, you marvel at the architecture, the sheer magnificence of this place, that is your sacred inner space.
- The Angelic choir is singing in the background, and you are drawn to the front of the building, near the altar.
- You sit down, listening to this inspirational sound.
- A fanfare announces the arrival of the Archangels Michael and Gabriel.
- You stand and welcome them in.
- They greet you, and thank you for coming to them this day, to work with them for the furtherance of humanity.
- Remember as you heal yourself, you heal humanity. These Illumined beings are wondrous, large in stature and colourful.
- Notice how they appear, for your journal later.

- Archangel Michael takes you by the hand and leads you through a large archway and gate to outside the cathedral walls.

- The entire entourage follow.

- He is guiding you down a path.

- He has heard your intention about your Inner Critic, and knows that somewhere down this path, your Inner Critic will be encountered.

- A being emerges from behind a large rock at the side of the path, and moves in front of you, holding a hand up in the air, as if to halt your progress.

- He/she is dressed in long dark robes, his/her face is hidden by a hood, which casts a shadow over the face. He/she is ancient, a visitor who is with you, and has been with you for aeons, since the Fall of humanity to the 3rd Dimension.

- This ancient pattern plays out in your mind with thoughts of scarcity and lack, of not being enough in every way. Instilling within you, a fear, a restriction. It is not for the likes of you to put yourself out there.

- This poor creature needs your love, your attention, affection and appreciation.

- In this moment, beloveds, you are being asked to take the hands of this being in yours and fill your heart with love.

- Breathe deeply, and make that wonderful Heart sound of 'Ah'.

- Direct it into the heart of this being. See his/her heart fill with the pure essence of love, until you are sure he/she feels forgiveness coursing through his/her body.

- Say with feeling, "I am willing to forgive you beloved, for holding me back, for sabotaging my efforts in this, and many other lifetimes, on all dimensions and time dimensions. It is now time for you to go back to the Light with Archangel Michael, in love and peace. Thank you for this soul lesson."

- As you finish, Archangel Michael takes him / her by the hand, and they float off to the Light, surrounded by a beautiful Violet Flame.

- Archangel Gabriel indicates that you must continue along the path, where you come to a beautiful ring of trees.

- The fairies of the glen are there to greet you with much excitement, as they have news of wonderful inspiring and motivational beings awaiting your presence. Here they are, all of your Inner aspects who today have been released to work with you, from this powerful moment, this moment of now.

- You are choosing to create your present and future reality right now.

- Please welcome your Inner Promotor, he/she acknowledges you with a beautiful smile, and shows you a book of suggestions as to how he/she is going to help you to promote yourself in the future if it is necessary.

- You are being asked to remember this list of information so that you can copy it down when you are back in the room with your journal.

- Next, your Inner Appreciator. He/she smiles with excitement as he/she shows you a list. A long list of all the wonderful attributes you have, that you haven't acknowledged in the past.

- He/she is going to remind you of them all, of how to be grateful for each one, and how to empower each one with Love and Light, so that they expand with joy.

- You are asked to copy the list down. You are seated and given pen and ink.

- You are amazed at the different things appearing. The fairies are sprinkling the list with magic dust, empowering and expanding the power of these gifts. They are singing and dancing around you as you find the inner gold and treasure hidden deep within you.

- Then, your Inner Lover floats in, the very essence of Love, surreal, intangible. This beautiful pink angel offers you a cup filled with a drink of pink essential "peace, and you are asked to drink it immediately. It tastes fragrant, floral as if you were drinking the scent of roses. You feel this essence course through your veins and body, loving every cell every tiny subatomic particle. You feel your entire four-body system responding positively to this life enhancing elixir.
  Her message is:

  "You haven't been able to see the beauty of yourself in the mirror. You've been looking in the wrong place. Look in to your eyes and deep into your heart".

- Next, your Inner Valuer comes in to the space. Quite a serious being, but with a soft touch, reminding you that, unless you value and appreciate who you are, nobody else will. When you remember who you really are, you will know that you need to choose to put yourself first, in a self-fulfilling way, throughout life. When you honour and respect yourself that way, others will do so too. Teach others how to treat you by showing them how you do it for you. Speaking your Truth is the first step on this course of honesty and integrity. He/she offers you a list of wonderful ways of valuing yourself. You are asked to write down all your gifts and talents. All the things that you find really easy to do, like reading and writing, singing, making up stories, performing, accounting, sewing, whatever it is for you. It is your inner strength, please value this now. Each one of us has unique strengths and gifts. Now take your list and simply blow your vibrant Heartsound all over the words, revitalising them with the sound of AAhh.

- Last but not least, your Inner Teacher arrives. The sage within you, who has all the answers and all the questions - the Seeker of Truth. This wise old being is graceful and peaceful. Quietly in the knowledge that he/she holds the keys the answers to all. He/she asks that you take the time for daily disciplines of meditation and contemplation. During these times, he/she asks you to visit with him/her, and ask whatever you need to know. He/she can access the libraries of the world for every answer. He/she can access the Soul DNA and the Akashic Records to find the answers to the questions. Infinite wisdom is yours at all times. He/she simply asks you to use his/ her abilities, to remember that they are there.

- You now take this opportunity to thank all these different aspects of you for working with you today. You wave them off as they disappear in a cloud of violet smoke, and you are left with your lists of 'things to do and be'. You lift them up, and with your guardian angel, you start coming back from this inspirational journey. You retrace your steps climbing back up into your heart centre and when you are ready, taking your time, being gentle with yourself bring yourself back to the room and open your eyes.

  Have a drink of water.

When you have adjusted to this dimension once again, write down what you need to in your journal from the lists. Add to that feelings and insights that came through for you.

Recapitulation

In this chapter, you have learned how to breathe from the cello belly and connect to your Heartvoice and make Heartsound. You have learned how to use it to heal yourself, by using it as a daily exercise. You have learned about the power of talking to your body in a positive way and naming our thoughts. You have looked at the negative programmes and patterns that can come in or that have been there for aeons. Most importantly, you have taken positive steps to changing the way you speak to yourself and others and released the Inner Critic. You have looked at the power of words and your name and you now know that you can choose to empower yourself and others simply by choosing your words carefully and mindfully.

As your body is almost totally water, remember it acts like a sponge for all that is said to it and felt by it. You can choose to expose yourself less to negativity in the media, TV in particular and negative toxic people and relationships in general.

All of this is essential to raising your vibrational frequency. Taking control and responsibility for your life, and choosing mindfully. Co-creating with Source a peaceful and harmonious earth experience in the Oneness.

'In the infinity of life where I am, all is perfect, whole and complete. I see any resistance patterns within me only as something else to release. They have no power over me. I am the power in my world.'

Louise L Hay, 'You Can Heal Your Life.'

Your Personal Re-calibration Plan

All blocks and patterns that are negatively affecting you are also lowering your vibration.

IDENTIFYING THE BLOCKS AND PATTERNS.

Step 1

Step one on your personal re-calibration plan is to identify the blocks and patterns that are present in your field.

Prepare to dig deep, have a really hard honest look at your life. Notice the patterns and blocks that continually reappear, even when you feel that you have done such a lot of work on them, they are still there. You may feel that you have patterns that simply kick in without conscious awareness from yourself. This may indicate the presence of an entity, a negative past life experience, an ancestral karmic pattern or a soul karmic pattern

Archangel Michael is devoting a lot of his magnificent energy at this time to helping individuals clear their past life issues from their molecular structure.

To do this, we will use a powerful, tried and tested meditation, which has amazing results to remove the strands, tentacles and source of these, and heal the four-body system.

Self created entities.

The power of focus and deliberate intention is well documented and written about. Whatever we focus our energy on, grows and expands. This is wonderful when we focus on positives, like our income. It begins to grow and expand. However, if we absentmindedly or unconsciously focus on not having enough, then, regrettably, that also expands, until that scenario becomes a concern.

Nothing we do changes the picture, because we keep re-enforcing the situation with our thoughts! We need to be ever mindful or consciously aware of what we are putting our thoughts to, and focus on what we want in our lives.

The way I see it in my mind's eye is like this - the first negative thought creates a small hole in the ground, and each time we repeat the thought, we plant the seed. We water it, and feed it, until after much fretting about it, we have grown a humungous great tree.

We have created an entity. A thing in its own right, which is growing bigger and bigger the more it is fed.

Having fed our monster, it now chooses to appear, and suddenly, we find that we have drawn our worst fear to us. We have become like a magnet.

When this happens over and over again, the entity has taken up residence, and becomes a pattern, an addiction, a habit.

We keep repeating the same old thing, making the same mistakes.

For example, having a relationship with the same kind of person over and over, e.g. a woman may find that her father wasn't available to her emotionally. She may begin noticing that she has married the same type of man as her father. Possibly, when she leaves that toxic unsupportive situation, she gets into other relationships that keep playing out like an old record. It gives her an insight into her relationship with her father. Whatever the pattern is, it will keep playing out until she rumbles it, then change and do something about it. In short, deal with it.

We are, after all, creating our reality from moment to moment, so, with that responsibility in mind, let us choose to create with care, and carve a masterpiece for ourselves.

I am going to ask you to focus on what it is that you want to heal in your life's experience. As this is a book about the voice and the throat, I am assuming that you will have, or have had a challenge in that area, so let us focus on that.

Perhaps you are an individual who:

- often gets sinus blocks.
- gets sore throats.
- has swollen glands.
- has thyroid issues.
- has a feeling of a lump in the throat.
- has something stuck in the throat.
- has difficulty swallowing.
- always has to clear your throat before speaking and or singing.
- finds your voice to be croaky or husky.
- feels yourself blushing when it's your turn to speak.
- is not good at speaking in groups.
- is not at ease (palpitations etc) when addressing a meeting.
- is fearful of expressing your Truth, your opinion.
- is lacking confidence and self-esteem.
- is afraid of your own power.
- who speaks very quietly or mumbles.
- who chokes easily on food or drink.
- is fearful of expressing your needs.

I am sure that I have not listed all of the scenarios that exist, so, please feel free to add your own, because I want you to focus on each of those and feel which ones resonate with you.

It can be useful to use a crystal to dowse for these answers, so that you can work on the ones that are not in your conscious awareness, as well as the obvious ones you know about, such as getting sore throats often.

You may be less aware that you have an underlying belief that it is dangerous to express your Truth.

If they resonate, simply tick the box.

As you do this, it will become apparent which of these, and there may be quite a few, that you, with the help of Archangel Michael are going to address and heal.

Creating a Sound Dome

When you have ticked all the boxes, I would like you to take sacred space, put on some beautiful day dreaming, relaxing music and engage in some delicious deep breathing.

Now we are going to create a SOUND DOME and do some work!

Meditation

- Take your awareness to your feet.

- See beautiful roots growing out of your feet and into the earth.

- Watch them as they burrow deep down to the centre of the Earth. Mother Earth invites you to put your roots into her beautiful beating heart. She loves you so much. She magnetises you to her surface.

- She feeds and nourishes your soul with the wonders of nature, your body with the produce of her soil, your mind with the stimulation of all your senses, your emotions by the healing of her waters.

- She asks you to drink of her healing ancient wisdom, and suck it up through your roots, until it reaches your feet. Each toe is filled with this golden nectar of life. It then comes into your feet.

- Flowing into the hip joints, the pelvic region and all the genital area, before it begins to climb and climb up the trunk of the body entering and filling every major organ on the way, until it reaches your heart.
- It fills your heart, swirling around it, relaxing it, inviting it to open and be receptive to this mystical and wondrous new energy.
- Breathe deeply, oxygenate the body fully at this juncture and deeply relax.
- Take your awareness to the crown of your head, and see it opening like a beautiful flower.
- Call forth from the Source of All that is, the beautiful and mighty Source Energy, and see it coming to you like a laser beam of amazing white light.
- The beam enters into the flower on your head and the energy releases into your brain.
- Allow this amazing Light to fill every cell, every atom in your brain. First, the left hand side, then the right.
- See both sides coming in to balance as you focus closely on the Light.
- It is flooding down your face now, into all the facial muscles. They are relaxing and letting go, as it reaches your jaw, you feel your jaw hanging loose and your tongue lying quietly on the floor of your mouth. Enjoy the sensation of peace and quiet.
- Allow the Light to flow down into your voice box and vocal cords, relaxing them, healing and making them whole. Feel the difference the presence of the Light is making.

- Allow the Light to journey on down into your lungs, cleansing them and re-coating them with this new energetic field. This Universal Energy is pouring into your heart, merging and mingling with your Earth energy.

- They begin to dance the sacred dance of Yin and Yang, balancing the energies, swirling like dervishes as they unite together.

- Send this newly created energy through every artery, every vein, every tiny blood vessel, until your body pulsates with this new vibrant energy.

- Send your new energy out in front of you as far as you can. Then, behind you as far as you can. Above your head as high as you can go, and beneath your feet as far down as you can go. Then, out to the sides, pushing out your boundaries, filling this energetic bubble you are forming with your new beautiful energy.

- Bring the colour pink, which has a very high vibration, into this bubble, and then begin to shape it into a beautiful dome.

- Mould the pink around it so it feels as if you are in a cocoon. You are safe, you are secure, and the sounds you make within this Sound Dome will resonate even more strongly and more powerfully within and around your body than they have ever done before.

- The sounds and the vibration will give every one of the millions of cells within your body a wonderful macro massage, revitalising and rejuvenating them.

Well done, this is your Sound Dome. A place of sanctuary and a place of amplification for your Heart voice and Heart sound.

To celebrate, take a deep breath, make all your connections and then sound Ahh three times.

Feel the resonance, the peace and the calm.

Within that safe place. Let your mind focus on the situation/s that you have identified. You might find it better to do this one at a time or all of them at once.

It is your healing session - do what feels right for you.

Begin by invoking the Power and Presence of Archangel Michael to stand beside you at this moment. Do this by simply saying three times,

"I invoke the power and presence of Archangel Michael to work with me in this moment, now."

Focus on the first scenario. Where in your body do you hold this feeling or sensation or physical challenge?

Take your awareness into that place. Does it have a colour, a texture, is it heavy or light?

As you take your total awareness into it, do you feel anything unusual, does a picture or vision present itself to you?

Whatever comes in, simply ask what the message is.

If it is a chair, for example, let it speak to you.

If it is a dog, colour or relative, allow them or it to speak.

DON'T edit what comes in. It may seem silly in your judgement, however, nine times out of ten, a big message will be contained in the words.

You may get nothing at all. If that is the case, simply thank whatever has come in for being there, and inform it that you are now going to heal this situation with the help of Archangel Michael, whether it participates or not, as it is time for it to go.

Ask Archangel Michael to help you let go, sever the ties, cut the cords, find the source and heal the energetic power leak to that situation.

He will also restore to you, the energy that you have already given away to that situation or individual.

You don't need to see the whole scene. Just know that all is being conducted for your highest good, and the highest good of all concerned. Remember as you heal - so does humanity.

As some of these situations will be from past lifetimes, acknowledge the fact that past life and ancestral healing is also taking place, and that your DNA structure is being restored.

Every time you do this healing sequence, a little more of your voice is restored, and more of your DNA.

Now, invite Archangel Michael to remove - from your throat and thyroid - any trapped energy or blocks that are not in your consciousness.

You will observe him removing black worm-like objects. Some of them long, some of them slimy and fat. All are being removed. Know this and feel this.

All the words you have ever stuffed down, not spoken out, suppressed or have had oppressed, which may have caused you to be depressed, are all going. They are going NOW.

Call forward the mighty Archangel Raphael to bring in his wonderful pink salve and bathe your throat and neck area.

He may need to delicately stitch your aura back together, where A.M. has removed the blockages.

He is surrounding you in a bubble of pink light and love, to expedite your healing process.

Take a deep and cleansing breath.

This part of the meditation is worth repeating over and over again.

Ask Archangel Michael to cleanse and clear your body of all negative cordlets that are around you.

You may feel him hoovering you and working in your aura.

Thank Archangel Michael and Archangel Raphael for their work and bid them farewell.

Repeat this part of the healing as often as you like, so that you deal with all of the scenarios that you identified.

Let me remind you that you are still sitting in your Sound Dome. I am going to ask you to find your Heartvoice, and make a Heartsound to seal your healing in today.

You will recall that we made a celebratory sound earlier on the upper level. This time, you will focus on sealing and healing the areas of the four-body system worked on.

But first, we need to find our way to the Inner Sound Dome.

- Take the key to the secret chamber of your heart and open the door, see before you the tri-fold flame. The part of you that is the All that is, burning brightly within your magnificent White Heart centre.

- Walk through the flame to the other side, and descend the steps in front of you.

- Go through a doorway there, and you will find that you are in your inner dome, the place where your Heartvoice lives.

Heartvoice

Remember this voice has been yours for aeons.

- Begin to gently allow your breath to deepen, and, when you are ready make the simple sound of 'AAH'. Allowing the air to simply flow through your vocal chords with little or no effort.

- Listen at the end of each sounding to hear or feel the other presence making this sound with you. The voice of the ancient sage within.

- Your focus of intention is that you are using your Heart voice to make the Heart sound required to seal in your healing.

(Notice for journalising purposes)

When you used your voice:

- Were there any changes?
- Did you need to clear your throat?
- Were you anxious to sound good?
- Is the lump still there?
- Did you feel inhibited?
- Had that feeling gone as you opened your lungs, and sounded your Heartvoice - making your Heartsound?

Awareness is everything.

- When you are ready, gently and slowly bring yourself out of the Inner dome, and through to the secret chamber.

Once again, enjoy the uplifting and cleansing enlightenment of walking through your inner flame.

- Close the door to your secret heart chamber. Lock it, and begin to focus on your breath.

- Come back into the room, stretch, have some water immediately and take your journal and pen and begin to write down your experience of that healing journey.'

Detoxification

Be prepared for a detoxification. When I first did this, I had a feeling of swollen glands for several days. Now, however, I very rarely get the sore throats or chest infections I used to get, only in times of major detoxification.

Allow 3 days for this healing to fully integrate into your system.

Drink a lot of water, I repeat, DRINK A LOT OF WATER.....

A brief recap

So far in this chapter, you have looked at the challenges in the throat chakra that have been manifesting in your life. You have created a Sound Dome to work in, and I will ask you to return to that safe place for doing all the work that you do. You have called upon Archangel Michael to work on the throat chakra with you. You have re visited how to make the Heartsound using the Heartvoice. You also need to undertake to do this exercise several times at weekly intervals, to get the most out of it.
You need to drink loads of water to help your body detoxify and be very gentle with yourself for the next few days.

STEP 2

Karmic Ancestral Patterning and Conditioning.

Take some space and time to relax

Breathing deeply, allow yourself to look at your life in a detached way, as an observer.

Notice repeated patterns in your life. The same sabotage coming in time and time again or the procrastination or the belief in lack or scarcity.

Write down all of your beliefs. Where did they come from?

Are they consciously yours or do you feel you learned them at the knees of your parents and grand parents?

You, in this moment, right now, are the sum total of your ancestral lineage, so whatever was experienced by them, whatever was believed in by them, is coming down your wires and playing out. When these patterns are still there it usually means that they are working through you from an Ancestral Karmic Pattern.

Session with Melinda

Melinda had noticed her pattern of always becoming involved with powerful men, who wooed her into relationship, and then became really abusive of her and her boundaries. In general, they were abusers of alcohol and sometimes drugs.
]
When we had our therapy session together, she had been to a family funeral earlier that day. Her grand mother had passed away at the grand age of 94.

Melinda was deeply concerned about her pattern. She really wanted to shift it and move on. She had found herself noticing all the Aunts that were there at the funeral. Powerful women in their own right. She knew that they had all married abusive partners. Then, with encouragement, she went back over her grand parents marriages and realised that both grandmothers had married alcoholics with the accompanying abusive behaviour. She wasn't clear about the Great grand parents, but agreed to investigate it with her own parents. She felt there was enough evidence of a pattern with the family knowledge she had.

She finally got it !! It was an ancestral pattern that had, and still was affecting her entire lineage, and making all of her attempts at having a loving and fulfilling relationship impossible. Her younger sister was in exactly the same situation. We worked on to do the visualisation that appears later in this chapter with amazingly powerful results.

Karmic Soul Pattern

We all choose what we are going to work on in our incarnations at the very beginning of our seeding on this life plane. We select the lesson that will keep reappearing in your lifetimes, until we have identified it, addressed it and healed it. This can, and does take many lifetimes. However, as Mother Earth makes her way towards ascension, so too are we being called upon to expedite our healing and address these issues. There is also no doubt that we are being asked to address all of this NOW. Not tomorrow, or next week or next lifetime but NOW. In order to support Mother Earth and her ascension, we too must heal ourselves, to ascend with her.

Once again, I would ask you to really focus and go within. What is your soul's pattern that needs to be healed? I know that my Karmic Soul Pattern has been a belief in scarcity, of not being enough or good enough. This has played through, and regardless of the work I have done on this, the remnants, until recently, have remained. I set my intention to completely heal and eradicate this pattern, this has been done, bringing a tremendous sense of freedom and liberation because now I

am free and totally energised to get on and complete my mission on this wonderful Earth.
Write down everything that comes in for you as you focus on what is your Karmic Soul Pattern. We will work on this in due course.

I also believe that we are the experiment rather than the experimenters. Suppose that we were infected deliberately at some point in time, perhaps generations ago, with addictions and the desire to self-destruct. Like a virus being placed in our genetic make up. How does that scenario feel for you? Listen to your body and your heart. Does it give you a 'yes' or a 'no'?

I say this, because addictions are humanity's greatest challenge, are they not ? Addictions can be anything; from addiction to life's dramas through to addiction to alcohol, sugar, caffeine, nicotine, drugs, your story, negativity, substances, fear, sex, people, adrenalin, eating, self-harming, lying, relationships and pain. Many of us have suffered from, or have at times, felt the urge to do away with ourselves. Indulging in the addictions which, if we work diligently at them, will eventually kill us and take us to the next dimension. Game over.

Take another moment to identify your addictions - people; places; things; situations; substances; career. Consider everything, and leave nothing out. All that you are attached to, or have an investment in. Write them all down. Also, write down the times when you have had the 'dark nights of the soul', when all had seemed hopeless and a strong desire had entered in to end it all.

There are those on this planet and in this galaxy, who have had a vested interest in keeping us in a state of fear and hatred. It makes us so easy to control.

By doing this work you will finally and totally lift all blocks, all barriers to this. You will find the voice of your heart and speak up and out. The least manifestation of this action is to get out and vote in your local elections because your voice will make a difference. From a place of integrity, and not ego, you may even feel the call to serve your country wherever it is in this way.

List your addictions here.

- ....
- ....
- ....
- ....
- ....
- ....
- ....
- ....
- ....

Remember the words of Ghandi.

'Be the change you would like to see in others - and in your country'

Prepare to change and make an enormous shift in your vibration towards ascension as you let go of lower vibrational patterns and addictions.

We are now going to do a powerful visualisation to help you deal with three issues.

Your Karmic Ancestral Pattern,
Your Karmic Soul Pattern,
Your Implanted addiction/s.

I will divide the meditation into three distinct sections, so that you can return to it many times if necessary, or you may just want to address one issue or segment at a time. You may wish to repeat any or all of it a number of times to ensure that all has been dealt with, that the source of the issue has been released, once and for all.

Meditation (CD track 3)

Take sacred space

Create your Sound Dome

When you are safely in your Sound dome, connect to your Heartvoice and your Heart Sound and make the sound of Ahhhh three times.

Keep your focussed intention on calming and settling yourself before this journey of illumination.

Take the key to the secret chamber of your heart and unlock it, see before you the tri-fold flame the part of you that is the Divine spark, the Divine light. Walk right through the flame to the other side allowing the flame to cleanse your four-body system in preparation for the work ahead.

You now see a beautiful gateway ahead of you and you enter through accompanied by your guardian angels and guides.

As you walk through, you come onto a landing and see a spiral staircase that is going down to a lower landing, deep within your inner world, your subconscious mind.

As you go down one step at a time, you go deeper and deeper within, and when you step down onto the lower landing once again you are guided to go through another gateway.

This time, it is a golden gateway, and it takes you directly into your own inner cathedral, which is a magnificent place, a place of the Light. It is the House of the Divine within you.

A round table can be seen to your right hand side with members of the Great White Brotherhood seated around it, The Keepers of your soul.

Akashic records and your soul DNA matrix are also there, although you cannot see their faces, as they are shrouded and silent.

Archangel Michael and his mighty army of spiritual warrior angels are on guard around your cathedral to protect you from outside interference.

You feel safe and secure and privileged to be in the presence of such Divine Beings. They are here to help you on your mission, to set yourself free at last from the bondage of Karma.

The Lords and Ladies of Karma join the throng and as the other myriads of Archangels and Angels of Love and Light and the Angelic Choir. Angels are saying, "we have to say there is standing room only in this place in your heart".

Sourcing and healing the Karmic Ancestral Pattern.

The Mighty Archangel Michael draws you forward to an energetic time line.

You are standing at the point of the present moment.

As you look to your right, you see the line extend a long way into the future, dividing off into lots of offshoots, the totality of the possibilities that exist within this lifetime for you.

As you look to your left, you see what looks like a vast and varied tree root system, going back and back in time, aeons ago, to when you first seeded on Mother Earth. You name, out loud, and with feeling, the ancestral pattern that you wish to heal on this occasion, and as you do so you see a light going on in amongst the filaments of the root system. It is winking at you, and it indicates the exact lifetime where this particular pattern started, and you note just how far back it is, as you look at it.

Archangel Michael is delighted to go in, and with his mighty sword, remove this block. He ensures that he removes all cords, ties and tentacles that are attached to it. Drawing it out by its roots and depositing it in a black bag, which he then gives to his Blue Angels, to take to the Light for transmutation. If you have more than one, and you wish to do the exercise again, please do so now.

When all is done, Archangel Raphael approaches with his pestle and mortar mixing up his beautiful pink concoction of unconditional love in the form of a healing salve.

He pours it over and in the wound, or wounds that are left. The job is done the entire Company of Heaven present in your Cathedral celebrate this as a job well done.

Sourcing and healing your Karmic Soul Pattern.

Now it is time to look in exactly the same way at your Light Body. If you are not good at visualisation, I don't want you to worry about this. I simply want you to know that, as you began to focus on your Karmic Soul Pattern, a light started winking on and off within your Light Body, and there may be more than one.

Allow Archangel Michael to go in and remove this pattern now, as this pattern is no longer required by you. You have learned the lessons and have completed the sacred contract. It is time for you to move on. You wouldn't have lifted this book had it not been time to finally resolve these issues. All is in Divine Right Order. If there are more, allow Archangel Michael to deal with them, and notice how Archangel Raphael comes in and heals afterwards with his amazing elixir. This pattern has now been removed. You may, or may not, be aware of what the pattern was about. The wonderful thing is - it doesn't matter one little bit. This works.

Sourcing and healing the implanted viral infection of addictions and self-destruct patterning.

Archangel Michael and his army of blue angels are surrounding you now. You feel the power of their magnificent energy, and as you are like a sponge, you are absorbing it now, into the deepest parts of your four-body system. As you do this, the places where these implants have been embedded become noticeable in your mind's eye. They may feel uncomfortable or painful, or they may make a sound or flutter or jump about. Whatever they are doing, they know the time has come for them to be sent back from whence they came, with Love and Light.

Archangel Michael takes his mighty sword, and inserts it into the places where the implants live. He is removing them now. Notice what you feel in your four-body system. His army of angels are escorting these out of your energy field and back from whence they came. This process continues until all four bodies are clear.

Great celebrations are now happening. The Angelic choir and the Angelic Orchestras are tuned in to you at this moment, and are singing and playing in concert to amplify and expand your energy field to its highest capacity. Celebration, as you lift your energy once again to a new calibration, a new frequency and sound. You join in with your own Heart sound and balance your entire body, bringing yourself gently and gradually to the room, when the time feels right.

You may feel very different as these various visitors and things have been with you a long, long time. Please allow a period of adjustment and integration. Be gentle with yourself and drink lots of water. Be aware of detoxification in all its different guises. Well done.

In Step 2, you have analysed yourself, and assessed what is going in your throat chakra. You have also looked at, and dealt with patterns and implants.

You should now be a lot clearer and lighter, and ready to move on to another level of healing and higher vibrational resonance.

Prepare to find your wings and strengthen them. Get ready to fly.

Your Re-calibration and Ascension plan

In chapter five, we dealt with the first two steps required to set you well on the path to raising your vibration significantly. In this chapter we are going to look at - remodelling the cells and chakras.

As we proceed along our ascension path, it becomes necessary to facilitate certain changes within our own cellular structure, so that we can cope with the extra Light that we are attracting and transmitting.

With the powerful, loving energies being directed to us from the Higher realms, the shape of our cells are changing from round to elliptical. We can expedite this by focussing on them and making our Heartsound into them. Our focussed intention being just that - to increase the amount of light capacity in our cells.

Visualisation

In your sacred space, close your eyes.

- Take your awareness to your breath and begin to consciously breathe into your cello belly, enjoy the richness of this feeling, allowing yourself to relax and let go, connecting to your inner space.

- Fill your specific intention with the desire to expand your cells with more light, and alter their shape, from round to elliptical. Your focussed intention becomes like the arrow on the bow set at its target.

- Begin to make your beautiful Heartsound, AAAhhh, vibrating the cells with it, growing them with love and light, seeing them change from round to oval.

- See each cell light up with joy, feel the shifts and changes happening and simply know that this change is taking place. Know that you have followed through with your visualisation, feelingisation and vibrationisation.

- Ask the cells to inform all of their brothers and sisters, as there are millions of them in your body, that miraculous changes are taking place for the benefit of all. Ask the key players to pass the word that they are changing and feel any discord turn to the most amazing harmony.

- Your actions are accelerating your ascension. You are becoming conscious Light and Love in action, well done.

- Take a deep breath and relax. Return to the room when you are ready.

You can do this exercise for as long as you like, making sure that you ground yourself afterwards, by putting your roots firmly into Mother Earth's heart and drinking some water. At least two glasses of water with a touch of lemon in it, if possible, to alkalise it.

Now we are going to look at remodelling the chakras.

These power centres are like spinning vortices in the body, and as you will see from the diagram, are placed at nine different locations on the body. As we remodel them, we are again opening the pipelines that will conduct more and more Light and Love through the body, accelerating the ascension process. Anything that is not of the Light will shift, so we need to be aware that what we are doing will release old stuck stuff, and that may cause a detoxification.

A word on detoxification

Just recently I worked with a client using voice and vibration techniques to clear old blockages and patterns. She experienced a dark night of the soul episode afterwards, when issues surfaced that she thought 'she had dealt with' years ago. She was angry that this work had disturbed it and brought it up again with such a lot of emotional charge. The fact is, the healing she had experienced in the past, had undoubtedly worked at a level, remembering that we are always peeling layers away.

The deep and incisive healing from the VIVA work had accessed the root or the source, of the problems and really brought it up to clear. Perhaps it was the trapped anger that released. Allowing emotional garbage to come up and then stuff it down again simply isn't going to work. It will remain with you, until you really do the final releasement - the letting go and forgiveness work.

If, as she thought, all the healing had been done, there would have been no emotional charge. She would have been able to view the issue in a totally detached way.

Therefore, I think it is important to be aware of the power of this work, and not to enter into it naively. When you choose to ascend and clear the four bodies, you are consciously choosing to get rid of anything and everything that is not congruent with the Light.

Let's get started. You need to take sacred space, and make sure that you will not be disturbed for at least one hour.

Meditation

- Take your awareness to your breathing, and breathe into the cello belly. This will be second nature to you now, and you will feel the grounding, centring and relaxing effect that this produces, as you find your core balance and alignment.

- To do that, focus on your spine and feel the connection, as you put a tap root down from the base of your spine into Mother Earth. Send the root right down into her heart, and feel rooted to her and loved by her.

- Now take a nice deep breath, and take your awareness to your crown. See a funnel or pipeline going from the top of your head to the Source of All That Is, so that you feel a strong connection there.
- You are now aligned to the Earth and the Stars.
- Feel your posture change, your spine lengthen, straighten and release as you breathe.
- Expand into that wonderful feeling. Breathe deeply into it, and then relax. Be like a sponge.
- Take your awareness to your Earth Chakra, which is about one foot beneath the surface of the ground. You have a beautiful sparkly crystal there, perhaps it isn't too clean, take this opportunity to cleanse it and clear it before beginning this work.
- Breathe deeply, finding your core stability. Tune into your heart, and find your Heartsound. Focus on cleansing, clearing, remodelling and expanding the earth chakra, so that it will channel more Light.
- With this in your awareness, begin to make the sound of OOOOHHHHH (as in choose).
- Make a deep, round, dark brown vibration, keep repeating this sound until your inner sage tells you that you have done it often enough. You will feel something shift. You may possibly experience a buzzing effect.

First – Base

- Repeat the same procedure, with the same focus and the same sound. Project that sound into the base of your spine. This time, making a deep rich red sound, filled with passion and inspiration.

- Stop when you are told to, by your inner promptings. Take time to notice the sensations and feelings experienced.

Second – Sacral

- The same procedure applies with the same focus. This time, the sound is AAAWWW (as in lawn).

- Make a deep, lush sound, feel the colour orange filling your senses. Keep going until you are told to stop, or feel a noticeable shift in energy.

Third – Solar Plexus

- The same procedure applies, the same focus and the same sound as last one, AAAWWW. This time you are a golden daffodil and you sound that experience into this centre.

- Keep going until you feel the shift, and are told to relax and move on. Listen to the inner promptings of your wise inner self.

Fourth – Heart

- Repeat the same procedure, with the same focus, which is a focus on cleansing, clearing, remodelling and expanding your heart chakra, so that it will channel more Light. With this in your awareness, begin to make the sound of AAHHHH, the sound of God, the sound of the Universe, the sound of effortless perfection.

- When you feel the desired change in vibration has taken place move on to the next centre.

Fifth – Throat

- Repeat the same procedure, with the same focus. With all of this in your awareness, begin to make the sound EEEEHHHHHH - as in feather.

- Fill your throat with the sound, relax in to it . Keep doing it as you bring the colour of bluebells into your visual awareness. Filling your throat with their wonderful colour and essence. When you feel the throat widen, expand and relax, then you can move on with confidence to the next centre, which is directly between your eyebrows.

Sixth – Third Eye

- Here we go again. The same set up procedure. Make sure your intentions are very clear, and begin to make the sound of 'EEEEEEE' - as in feel, focussing on the area right between your brows.

- Visualise the colour of mauve along with your sound, and allow it to clear and expand this centre. Well done, you will have a sense of clarity, as all the clutter of the mind begins to dissolve and float away. When it feels right, move to the next centre.

Seventh – Crown

- You are well used to the set up for all of this, so without prompting, you can immediately begin to focus the sound of 'EEEEEEEE' to this centre.

- See the crown in your mind's eye begin to open and clear. See your satellite dish come out of the top of your head, to transmit and receive more clearly.

- See the dish revolve around, sending and receiving its message, bringing in golden and silver light to cleanse and clear it.

- Keep making that inspirational sound as spirit communicates with you. You may feel yourself downloading information into what are now very clear chakra pipelines.

- Remember what you are being given in this moment. Move on to the next centre when you feel ready.

Eighth – Soul Star

- Stay with the uplifting vibration and sound of EEEE. You will notice that this is a very stimulating sound. When you focus on cleansing and clearing this centre, please invoke the Violet Flame to come in to clear this chakra as well as the rest of your system.

- See it flash around you with violet, gold and silver Lights, burning away the last vestiges of anything that is not of the Light. Your sound is becoming clearer and clearer as you become aware of the inspirational material held within this centre. This is your energy blueprint centre, all that you are, all that you will be is held here. Celebrate as you see it spill over and out, making its way down into your other chakras.

- Bring all of this potential into your heart and dowse it with unconditional love. Bring it into your solar plexus, to instil the will power required in order to manifest, and into your sacral, to find the enhanced creativity you need to ground and deliver your star material. Now, take it into your throat centre, where it will become the words, the songs, the healings, the vibrant sound of creation itself for you to communicate to the world.

- This is very powerful stuff, so enjoy the feeling of inspiration and wholeness, of total connectedness to Spirit, to God to the Oneness with every thing.

Grounding

- Make sure that you ground yourself before returning to the room by putting your roots down into Mother Earth and securing yourself there.

Protection

- Protect yourself, by asking Archangel Michael to put his deep blue cloak around you. See yourself zipping it up.

- Now place mirrors all around you with the mirror side facing OUT, so that if anything is directed at you from the dark, it will simply bounce right back to its source. Anything of the Light, however, will come through, because you are open to receiving Love and Light in abundance!

Gratitude

- Well done, have a drink of refreshing water and have a good look round at all the treasures and abundance in your life that are all around you, and thank the powers that be that life is so good to you in every way possible.

With the Chakras balanced, we are moving on to the Axiatonal Lines.

Activating the Axiatonal lines.

Our axiatonal lines have been de-activated over lifetimes, since the Fall. They lie dormant, ready for re-activation. The time to do that is now. When you learn how they can increase your Light quotient, you will understand that they are vital to your Ascension.

The Axiatonal lines link to your acupressure points, and through those, to the meridian lines in your body. As you reactivate them, they will become an all powerful conduit of Light to your energy circuits, and will of themselves, bring more Light into your being than is possible by any other route - and that includes the Crown Chakra. They will broaden the pipelines that you will channel the Word through, making your unique resonational sound.

As you open and use the Axiatonal Lines, so you are able to sound even more of yourself than you did before, bringing more of yourself to this wonderful party that we call LIFE.

To reactivate the Axiatonal lines, you simply need to take sacred space for 10 minutes once a day, or add this process on to your existing Heartsound practice, chakra balancing and meditation discipline.

Re-activation

- Focus your attention on your breathing, enjoy the relaxation, the quiet and calm you are inducing simply by breathing deeply and regularly.

- Feel every muscle respond lovingly and let go of its held tension. As you soften and sink even deeper into your sitting bones, you ground yourself.

- Find your core balance and prepare to focus your attention on your Axiatonal Lines.

- As you view your four-body system in your mind's eye, you can see clearly or imagine the Axiatonal lines spreading out from the body, looking forlorn, shrivelled and undernourished.

- Begin to breathe into them, see them begin to plump up and out, as new life is poured into them.

- Find your Heartsound. We are simply going to hold the intention of reactivating these lines as we make the sound of AAhh as often as you feel necessary.

- Watch the changes taking place, feel them, hear them. Notice how they change. You are in charge of your life, your four-body system and your Axiatonal lines. Whatever you decree will come to pass.

At the end of the first session simply decree the following.

"I decree that the Axiatonal lines around and connected to my body are now fully reactivated and operational. And so it is." (Three times).

Bring yourself back to the room.

I would ask you to repeat this exercise every day for one week, although you do not need to repeat the Decree. Divine Intelligence will hear it the first time.

Becoming the conduit for the Divine voice of Mother/Father God.

All of the above exercises are designed to strengthen your Light body and open your channels of communication, so that you receive and transmit more Light. You will also allow more space for the Divine Voice of Mother/Father God to speak and communicate through you. This could be a subtle difference to the tonal resonance of your voice, which will be available to all who come into contact with you.

As Lightworkers, we have always known that our presence in and of itself is healing. Now, we have the added advantage of consciously knowing that the Divine is communicating through us as well.

The Divine or Spirit offers the right words to be spoken at the right time. I'm sure we have all had the experience when we have wondered, having spoken some words to a client, group or friend, 'where exactly did that come from?'.

This phenomenon will now become the order of the day, because, as you learn to accept and amplify what you are receiving, you will learn to get out of your own way. That is to say, the Editor in your left brain will go on holiday, and you will be aware if he pops back to open some mail.

Hand your communications over to Spirit. Find your Heartsound before you open your mouth. Life will improve a thousand-fold. Become an inspirational channel for Source.

Bridge

Some people like to put a bridge in. An example of that would be, a friend of mine who makes a clicking sound before channelling, so that it is clear to listeners when she is directly channelling. This bridges from Spirit to the Listener.

This is fine and right for some, however, I believe that people will know anyway when you are channelling, because they are receiving a particular resonance through your voice that is on a higher dimension. They will simply know that you are speaking the TRUTH, - always the Truth, with a velvet gloved fist, when it is necessary to deliver a lesson of love. Because that is what life is about, learning, growing and developing in LOVE. That is who you are - at the end of the day. You can do it!

People frequently deny their innate abilities to tap into Source and Spirit. You have just been given ways to really amplify and expand these abilities. Use them, and things will change significantly.

Everyone can do this, it is about Trust and Faith. It is also about listening to your gut, your inner knowing; allowing your discernment and integrity to guide you through.

Anything that emanates from Spirit or the Divine, will be positive, given in love, for the highest good of you - and all concerned. If at anytime, anything negative enters in, then you need to check out who that source is, by dialoguing with it. If, after three challenges, it still remains, and I doubt if it will, then you need to ask for clarification and verification. If you continue to feel uneasy on any level, command it to go back to the Light for transmutation with Archangel Michael. Listen to your inner physical promptings. They are usually spot on.

The Light has already won, and, as a Spiritual Warrior, working with Archangel Michael, you are divinely guided in right action, every way, in what you say and do. So listen, listen, listen and get out of your own way.

As you become a clear conduit for the Light and Source, you become an ascended healer and mentor. Your powers of healing for yourself and others are enhanced beyond belief. Take the time to do these exercises and note the changes.

Take time right now to note down anything that has come up to challenge or inspire you during this chapter.

"There are many paths to the Light, all sacred, all meaningful, choose the one for you that makes your heart sing."

Patricia Iris

Polarity and Patricia's Passionometer

The Universal laws of polarity are well known. We live in a world of Light and Dark, Good and Evil, Yin and Yang, Male and Female, Love and Hate and so on and so forth. This duality exists in all of creation; one cannot exist without the other.

By using this understanding, we can see that Life flows between two extremes of different vibrations. We can take control and choose to sail through life on an even keel as it were, because we can choose to shift and change where we are, at any time, on our scale of vibrational polarity.

Let's look at different scenarios that we may wish to change or improve in our lives.

Have a look at the Passionometer on the page below.

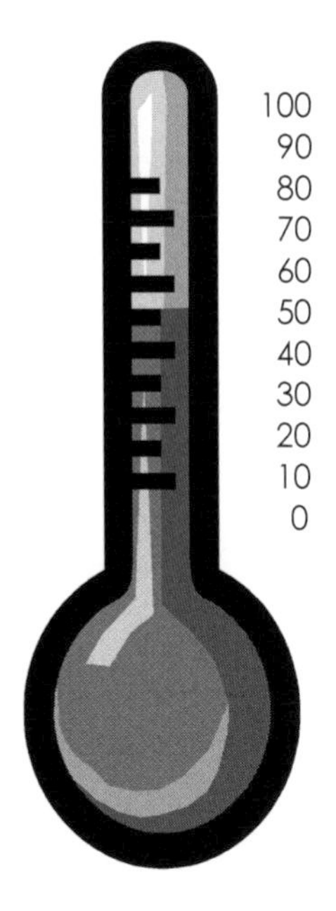

You will see that it is marked clearly from 0 through to 100. The base, which is bulbous, contains a dark red liquid. You are going to use that liquid as your moveable mass when you focus on it.

Perhaps you might like to photocopy the Passionometer and place a few on one sheet.

Suggested headings to work on could be:-

- Poverty to Wealth.
- Illness, disease, discomfort through to Total Health.
- Depression and unhappiness through to inspired and happy.
- Spiritually bereft to spiritually connect to Source.
- Absence of self love through to total self love and appreciation.
- Guilt and shame through to freedom and love.
- Apathy, through to passion and desire.

(Feel free to add as many as you like).

Mark on your sheet where your energy is currently resonating. For example, your self-love may be quite good, but not great.

- Close your eyes, align yourself by breathing relaxing and settling down.

- Allow your right brain to come in with the right number for you between 0 and 100. Remember, no editing. Give yourself permission to trust that your inner wisdom is coming up with the right number, right now.

- Put a mark at the number on your Passionometer.

For our example we will say that your self-esteem is resonating at the number 50.

- Now, taking sacred space, you can choose to either focus on the paper and the drawing, or you can close your eyes, and visualise the tube and the bulb at the bottom, filled with that delicious liquid.

- Begin by taking deep breaths into your cello belly to oxygenate and relax, then return to normal breathing.

- Connect with your Heartvoice, make your Heartsound of AAHH - effortless perfection, the sound of Mother /Father God, and focus into the bulbous part.

- Your intention to raise your self-esteem is like a penetrating laser beam. As you harness your empowered intention through the sound, observe the liquid as it begins to bubble up with this new energy.

- Keep doing this, feel the energetic shifts within you. Deep breaths and deep empowering sounds are lifting your energetic vibration to new levels, changing your energy blueprint forever.

- When the time is right, stop the sound. Listen for a moment to the sound of silence, and take your awareness to your heart.

- What is the number of the reading that is coming up for you now? Mark it on your sheet.

You might like to keep going until you reach your goal, which may or may not be 100. Whatever your chosen goal is, when you are there, slide the holding bar up to that point and lock it there so that it holds. For maintenance of this, all you need to do is to go in daily and ensure that the level is still where you want it, and if it is not - you know what to do. Make your Heartsound into it until your self-esteem rises once again.

I feel we need to <u>really</u> monitor our self-esteem, and keep working on it, as simply living a human life at this time exposes us to many negative things that we are not necessarily conscious of. It is your responsibility to keep yourself in balance and clear.

We also need to be aware that as we have shifted energy, there will be a detoxification of the blockages. They will manifest in many different ways, as I have stated in previous chapters, so be aware!

Taking time

Obviously, doing these exercises takes time to do, and often workshop participants and clients, will say to me that they don't have time to meditate or do exercises like this.

I feel that attitude is almost madness, because these are the very disciplines that will keep you calm, peaceful and fully balanced to deal with the rigours of the daily life in the 21st Century, which for some, is extremely demanding.

You are in charge of your diary and schedule. So, create a healthy one, with time for you. Include all the things you love to do and be and, at the same time, honouring the responsibilities you may have to work, clients, students etc. Yes, it may mean getting up a little earlier, or going to bed a little later. However, you will be living life to the full, participating and contributing on all levels, and you will feel incredibly engaged and energised by that.

Anything else is giving your power and authority away to other people, and the world around you - and that is totally dis-empowering. You are responsible, you are in charge, and it is down to you. Take control NOW and yes, it may mean saying NO to people and not being on call to all the people, all of the time. The greatest challenge you face is dealing with your immediate family in this way. It can be done, and when done, gives them the gift of a shining example of self-empowerment in action. They will then demonstrate that in <u>their</u> lives too. Remember what you do for your highest good is for the collective's highest good as well. 'One for all and all for one'.

This is the call. 'Put yourself First'.

This is not what we were conditioned to do, however, we and our ancestors got that one all wrong. Only by doing just that, and really loving yourself, will self-empowerment become a reality for you and others around you as you lead by example.

As you can see, using the Passionometer can make huge shifts to your energetic blueprint. We can also use it for manifesting; ways of being, prosperity and abundance.

For example, you may have it in your awareness that you are pretty critical and judgemental of yourself. It is in your awareness, so you take active steps to remedy this self-abuse if it comes in.

Regrettably, if you are like that about yourself, you are probably like that about others as well. When you catch yourself doing it, these are the times when your ability to see God or the Light in yourself, or indeed the other person, has temporarily gone. You have stopped unconditionally loving and accepting.
Awareness is everything!

Affirmation

"I am love in action right now"

What a wonderful affirmation! How can we really energise that? and, make sure that at every moment of every day, that is what we are doing.

We are going to consciously implant this affirmation into our entire being with the use of the Passionometer.

- Close your eyes, breathe deeply into your cello belly, find your core alignment and balanced stability.

- You are feeling strong and centred. There is nothing on this planet that you cannot achieve, and getting rid of this judgement and critical pattern is going to be easy.

Visualisation

- See yourself in your laboratory. You are the chief magician in your village, town or city.

- Take the words, 'I AM LOVE IN ACTION RIGHT NOW' and write them down, using a wonderful deep red ink on beautiful paper. Scrunch the paper up, and drop it into the Passionometer.

- As it reaches the wonderful liquid at the base, you notice the paper with these words written on it, dissolving into the mass of energy there.

- The liquid burbles and bubbles up, rising up and up the tube, until it registers 100. The whole tube is now full up with this empowering affirmation.

- Find your beautiful Heartsound and make the sound of AAHH into it. Sending it the Love and Light from the Illumined Beings of Light, who are channelling through you. They are empowering your voice with a special resonance and tone. You can hear this special tone and you feel like you are being sung.

- Your liquid is now ready to drink. Pour it into a large glass. Listen to it as it tinkles into the glass.

- Take it to your lips, and now, feel yourself drinking it down. Taste it. it is sweet and delicious. The beautiful smell of this elixir is pervading the room you are in, and your body is like a sponge absorbing it. Every cell, every atom, every subatomic particle is filling with this message. I AM LOVE IN ACTION RIGHT NOW.

- Notice how you feel. Prepare to write it down when you come back to the room, which you are going to do right now, after you have thanked all the Illumined Ones who have been facilitating your healing.

- Take a few deep breaths and come back to the room.

Take a few moments to write down how you experienced that visualisation.

This technique can be used for a myriad of purposes. You can drink a cup of protective elixir or healing, for specific ailments. If you wish to bring a certain colour and its qualities into your field, then drink that too. Always call upon the Illumined Ones to guide you, and then, you cannot go wrong. This is such a good technique. It is effective, and it is limitless. You can dream up lots of different scenarios as you are the most effective healer and magician in your life, are you not?

"As within so without, as without so within"

Anon

Metaphysically Clearing Your Vibration

Your car and your house are reflections of you. In other words, your outside world reflects your inner world. The longer you have your house and your car, the more they become imprinted with your vibrational field. They resonate with your vibration and frequency, and are just as much a part of you as your nose or hair. Using these effective mirrors can bring you limitless metaphysical information on your well being at every level of your energetic field.

Answer the following questions honestly, jot them down in your journal.

- How tidy is your car?
- Is it in good running order?
- Is the paintwork clean and in a state of good repair?
- Does the colour of your car make your heart sing?
- Do you feel it is time for a new car?
- Is the battery well charged of have you let it run low?
- Is there plenty water in the radiator and windscreen washers?
- Do the wiper blades work well?
- Is the heating working efficiently?
- Are all the wheel bearings operating smoothly and soundlessly?
- Is the interior furnishing clean?
- Is the fuel tank full?
- Does your radio and CD/tape player function well? Do you use it?

Let's see how you got on with this.

- If your car is tidy and well kept inside, then you are probably a well organised methodical person. If it is not, then you possibly have a lot on your mind, feel overwhelmed and never very clear about your decisions with a leaning towards procrastination.

- If your car is in good running order, then you are probably healthy with a good regime of exercise and diet. On the other hand, if your car has one or two things wrong, then it is equally possible that you are not 100% health wise either. Notice the ailing parts and equate them to the equal parts of your body to find the message for you.

- If your paintwork is clean and intact i.e. no bumps and lumps, then you are probably very conscious of how you present yourself, and do it well. Any defects on the outside, especially if they have been there for a long time, reflect a more laid back attitude to this, verging on not really bothering with how you look. This reflects low self-image and prosperity issues.

- If you love the colour of your car, then this is wonderful, as you will be pulling that colour in from the Cosmo, and that colour will be working on your energetic field positively, as that is the colour vibration that you need right now. If on the other hand, you are yearning for something else, then you have moved on.... In need of another colour.

- If you feel it is time to renew your car, then this is a sign that you have let go at a significantly deep level, and are ready to step into a new way of being. Take a moment to note down all the times you have changed your car, and notice when that occurred. Notice how it heralded a new you, a new way of being, a new level of prosperity or spiritual way of living.

- The battery in the car simply reflects how much energy you have stored. I can remember being in Kuaii, Hawaii, with my friend, Linda Miller, as we attended our Louise L Hay Advanced teacher programme. We had hired a car, and were taking time off to visit Serge Kahili King, Author of

The Urban Shaman and Tom Carpenter who is a teacher on 'The Course on Miracles'. The car would not start, the battery was dead. This reflected Linda and I, as we were both seriously tired, however, perseverance got the car going, and we went to the seminars. The mechanic told Linda that she must have left the lights on overnight, and that was why the battery was so low. This simply wasn't the case. She hadn't done that. The car was coming out in sympathy with us, and reflecting our tiredness and lack of energy.

- If you run out of water in the radiator or washers then this is a reminder to you to drink more water. As we have already discussed we are 85% water. The rest is oil, so make sure your personal oil level is up as well. Omegas 3 and 6. That way, any minor ailments, aches and pains disappear and energy rises significantly.

- Wiper blades are like our eyes and vision. If they are in good condition, they clear away debris well, and we see clearly. If they need to be renewed or straightened, then this reflects a need in you to have your vision checked, and/or to focus on your third eye when working with the Archangels - asking them to clear your clairvoyance channels.

- Heating problems may reflect your inability to keep your circulation up to par. Look at ways of improving this by exercise, and be aware of what you are eating. Warm nourishing soups full of vegetables are great for restoring the circulation balance. While training people in Reiki, I often hear that feet are the cold parts, the extremities that didn't warm up. That could be the case pre Reiki, après Reiki, the channels are usually well opened, and warmth is not a problem, even in the outposts of the body. Check for anaemia too, a good vitamin and mineral can help to solve this problem easily.

- Wheel bearings and links are all to do with the hips and knees, and it is all about going forward. This type of malfunction in the car could herald the need for you to look at where you are resisting moving forward fearlessly. Call Archangel Michael in to help with strength and courage, ask him to help you deal with the fear, and be open as to how he intends to do that. Be open and receptive to receiving all good into your life. Wear Red, it will keep you balanced and grounded and energise you too.

- Keeping the inside of the car clean, simply reflects how clean your insides are and how clean an eater you are. If you are avoiding mucous forming foods, such as wheat and dairy, and also avoiding red meat, then you are eating cleanly. It is simply a case of looking at it all with new eyes. Do eat for health and what makes you feel good. Memories around food like 'my mother used to make an apple pie that was to die for' creates an endorphin rush within you, because as you eat, you are recalling that good feeling. Watch the quantities, you can still have all of that fun and good feeling from half the amount you usually eat. Notice what you are eating. Notice the gungy sauces etc. Ask yourself, "do I need all of this ?" Listen when your body tells you the answer. Do eat with your eyes. If you feel good about what you are eating, you are healing yourself. Relish the colours of your food. Relate them to the chakra colours, and you will notice then what is going on for you, which parts need energising.

The power of the mind harnessed to the power of the voice, the spoken or sung word, can help you release excess weight easily and safely. Have a look at the last paragraph in this section to find out how.

A regular clean out of the car is great for the care and clearness of your mind, and reminds you to detox your body at least twice a year. There are loads of books available on that, and you should give your liver a boost by finding a detox that suits you.

- Keep your tank full up. By eating well and cleanly, drinking lots of water, sleeping, exercising, stretching, laughing, meditating and sounding, you will keep your energy levels up. Your tank will be full of high vibrational energy.

- Is your sound centre switched on? As described in previous chapters, we know that sound harmonises our entire field of consciousness. I have always used my car as a University. I have learned to use it as a sound dome as well. This we can do in two ways.

First of all, choose carefully, prior to each journey, the kind of music you want to listen to. Choose something that you love, that is inspirational and happy. When you get to your destination that is the way you will feel.

Perhaps you prefer to listen to a motivational speaker such as Dr Wayne Dyer or Anthony Robbins. You will jump out at the other end - totally energised and inspired. Don't, however, listen to anything that induces an altered state such as trance or high-powered relaxation. That would be dangerous for you - and everyone else on the road.

The second point would be that you can make your own sounds. You can practice Heartsound and Heartvoice in the car, and notice how it keeps you calm as you drive through the traffic. You can practice balancing your chakras by toning in to each one. You can balance and clear your spine, one vertebra at a time and your organs, one at a time. Jonathan Goldman one of the foremost sound healers on the planet at this time, recommends different sounds and tones and notes to use for specific healing access.

If you have a tape or CD of these, then use it, if that rings your bells. You may wish, as I do, to use your own intuition, listen to the sound sage within and whatever note or tone that you are given, will be the right one for the occasion, and the healing required. Trust and Faith are the two great elements here, and as I know these things simply work - and work simply, that is the bottom line for me. IT WORKS.

Well there we go, you thought you just had a car that gets you from A to B. Here it is, your very own metaphysical information and healing centre. I have my own little blue car on the market just now, as I simply need to do red. Wear it, feel it, eat it, drink it, share it, speak it and sound it. 'Simply Red', I think someone has already used that name!!

Archangel Raphael is the Archangel who will protect and safeguard your journeys, and the vehicle you travel in. Remember to bring his energy into your car. See a green light pervading every cell, every atom in the car. If you can visualise it to be like a glass car, then imagine it filling up with green living high frequency light - Archangel Raphael's healing colour. St. Christopher is awaiting your call to ensure that you have a safe journey so remember to invite him in as well.

Affirmation

"I am surrounded by wonderful, careful and competent drivers, all is well everything in my life's journey is as it should be, I am safe. And so it is."

Your House.

I am going to use the same metaphysical logic, (if that isn't a contradiction in terms), to look at your house.

Your house and everything in it, reflects you and your vibrational field of consciousness. So, let's have a good look inside it to see what is going on.

Answer these questions, perhaps jot the answers down for future reference.

- Do you like your house? Do you like where it is, the town, street, position?

  If the answer is yes, that's good. If not, then where would be the ideal place for you?
  Write down what would really make your heart sing as regards location.

- Do you like the style of house e.g. bungalow, villa, terraced or apartment?
  What would your dream house be like perhaps you already own it, perhaps not.
  Write down what your heart is telling you right now, be descriptive, have fun.

- Is it <u>your</u> house or are you renting? Are you living in what was a matrimonial/previous relationship house for you or your partner/husband/wife?
  If it is your house then fine, you probably chose it with your partner, or for your own occupation. If that is not the case, if you have moved in to what was a matrimonial or previous relationship home, how do you really feel about that? Do you feel that the energetic imprint of the previous partner, husband or wife is still around? If so, do you need to speak up about moving on, or choose to do your best to cleanse the place of the past and all that the past means?
  Write down how you honestly feel.

- Is the exterior and grounds/garden in good condition, neat and tidy?
  Is this the right space for you to connect to nature and honour the wildlife. Does it have a colourful pallet of

flowers and trees? Is all neat and tidy? Do you feel the presence of the Nature Spirits and Fairies? Is there a sacred space for you to 'be' and commune with them? If it is a lofty situation, do you have a good view or are you hemmed in. How do you feel about that?
Write it down.

- Is the house in a light or dark position? This is simple. You will either feel light and airy, or overshadowed by trees and perhaps other buildings. How does it feel - uplifting or down heartening?

- When you enter into your house, how does it feel energetically?
  Is it clear / clean?

- How does it smell? Is it welcoming and warm or cold and foreboding?
  Dampness and cold can indicate energetic work needing done, as well as practical alterations or fixings needing attention. Tune in to your heart, and allow your right brain to give you the answers required. Trust your intuition. It might not be what you are expecting. Play music to do this, it helps you to bypass the left brain and ego.

- The kitchen, the heart of the house, is it warm? Do you feel cosy and nourished, or is it cluttered and packed full of stuff, food, ironing, papers.
  Take a look at your heart, if there is clutter in this room then it is the same in your heart space and arteries. Energy and blood must be able to flow freely. Keep surfaces clear and clean. What do you need to do to achieve a clear space.
  Write it down.

- Are the cupboards filled with lots of lovely foods that you enjoy, or full of mistakes that you allow to accumulate ?, until there is no room left to put new things in, like herbs and fruit teas. I once had a great desire to buy these, but didn't drink them much, because I prefer green tea. Instead, I hoarded them. What are you hoarding in your cupboards? Do a critical analysis on the contents of the cupboards, and fridge. What do you need to do, to be sure that you are unclogging your arteries?

- How is the kitchen decorated. Are you pleased with it, or does it need revamping? It might be dull and a bit sad, in need of some joy and happiness. Get a colour chart from the local paint shop, and be innovative in the new colours to bathe your heart centre in.

  Write down what you intend to do. If you like it the way it is, well, that's great!

- How about the floor? Do you keep it crisp and clean, or could it do with a new carpet or tiles, or even just a good brush and wash. Be honest, have a good look at it. It represents foundations and groundedness.

- The lounge, your place of relaxation and home entertainment. Is it a place of peace and content, or are there things lying about that could be cleared?
  Do you have clean lines or are you over endowed with things - 'objet d'art' - from bygone days. Do you need them? Do you use them? Do you love them? If that is a 'NO', then let them go!
  Is the energy crisp and clear? Does the paintwork need freshened up, or is all pristine. The corners - are they dark and stagnant, or enlivened by mobiles or lights?
  The furniture and carpet, is all in good condition, smelling good and dust free? Are all your books, magazines, CDs, tapes, videos and DVDs carefully filed, or lying about in heaps?
  Is there sufficient lighting in the room? Are your curtains what you really want, or have your tastes changed in recent weeks, months, years?

- Your bedroom, your place of rest, calmness, perhaps meditation.
  Does it reflect the sacred space that you deserve when you close your eyes at night, or is it surrounded by books, clothes lying about on chairs, dirty cups from early morning cuppas, shoes abandoned carelessly, not to mention smelly socks? Notice what is hanging around in, what could be, the calmest room in the house. If you are in relationship, it is also the place of physical love and passion with your partner, wife or husband. Are the bedclothes clean and soft, comfortable and cosy? Is it the love nest that you would want to have in this romantic situation?

- The bathroom/toilet, your letting go room. Your place of elimination and detoxification. Is it cluttered with all kinds of beauty and hair products, which are packed with all kinds of harmful chemicals? Harmful to your wellbeing, and harmful to the environment when they are flushed down the loo or the sink. Conscious awareness in all things, is required to help heal Mother Earth. There are many wonderful products available on the market that are eco conscious and eco friendly. I humbly suggest that for your body's sake and the planet's sake, you convert to them - as quickly as you can.

- The office. Is it neat, tidy, clutter free? If it is not, you will no doubt feel weighed down mentally,. Your brain tired out with the mass of subjects pulling at your energy for attention. Take control today, and go through the piles of stuff. Be bold! Be hard. If you haven't looked at it in the last year, then throw it out, or shred it, or take it to the recycle place. Keeping this space clear reflects a clear mind, free of extraneous thoughts, and free to be creative in lots of different ways. Freedom!

  It is the same with your computer, regularly go in and clear out old emails and files that are no longer being used. You really don't need to keep everything from years past.

This will help it to function quickly, and boot up faster as well. If you need to be sure, to be sure, as they say in Ireland, you can copy everything to a disc before deleting and then you can keep the disc somewhere safe.

How do you speak to your computer? Do you think it is happy to be your computer? People sometimes shout at their computers and printers in frustration. They too are part of you. You are really just berating yourself. All of these wonderful technological aids are only as good as those operating them, unless they have a virus. Having a virus equates to you having an entity, or some other uninvited pattern or visitor invading your space. So look at it on all levels. Life is intriguing and mysterious when you view everything as a message, a teacher. Then you can adopt a lighter attitude to it all.

By now, I think that you are getting the idea of this exercise. It is about taking a look at every room in the house. Is it free from clutter? If not, have a good clear out. Throw things away or sell them. Have a car boot sale or a garage sale, and raise some funds for something you have been dreaming about getting.

Renew carpets or curtains that have served their time, with new fresh vibrant colours. Whatever it is for you, do it now, don't wait. if you have the money, that's great. If not, come up with innovative ideas to raise some cash. Make it your priority to renew and lift the energy in your living space. Make sure you are living in a home that reflects who you are, and it will lovingly respond by feeling totally different and attracting new energy in to you on all levels. You will feel lighter and energised as a result of this exercise.

Abuse or neglect the space, and you, at some level, are doing the same to yourself. Allowing it to get unacceptably dirty, reflects low self-esteem and self-worth. Learning how to really love yourself is therefore the top priority for you, start by loving the space you live in.

Make a list right now of all the things you can do in your house to unblock its energetic blueprint. This will allow the energy to flow through your house unimpeded. It is the premise that the Chinese discipline of Feng Shui is based on.

Ideas for your list are:-

- Clothes you could send to charity.
- Out of date foods in cupboards.
- Unused items that someone else could benefit from.
- Books to libraries or friends who might enjoy them even benefit learn and change their life from.
- Paint a room or two bring in the new colours you feel drawn to.
- Renew curtains.

Write it all down now. Don't stop until you have listed at least 20 things to be done.

Your body will respond as you change your house. It is your house also. Perhaps your body is also suffering from convenience eating - processed foods and quick meals taken on the run. Learn to love cooking. Taking your time and mindfulness to prepare a meal or at least some part of the meal.

Using Heartsound in the House.

Food.

Make Heartsound into the food as you prepare it.
Focus your intention on blessing the food, empowering it with love, giving thanks for the food and thanks for the little things in life. Make the sound of 'Ahhh', the sound that connects and merges you with the Divine. As that vibration enters the food, it will become even more delicious, nourishing and supporting of you than it did before.

Remember to do this, it is so simple, the food will taste different, as it lets go of any fears that it has picked up before it arrived on your table for consumption.

Drink

The same applies to anything you drink. Make a Heartsound into it. Mindfully bless it, send it love and gratitude, and know that, as you do that, it is responding in amazing ways, by changing into harmonious shapes at a cellular level. As you drink, you are drinking with awareness and you are drinking in pure LOVE.

Organic and eco-friendly

Organic food is the most nutritious. Whenever possible, use it along with eco-safe products. Our planet is important. il it isn't here, we are not here. It is as simple as that. So what you do now will affect your descendants - BIG TIME, so now is the time to get your act together.

Plumbing and Electricity

Waterworks

Any problems with your water works in the house, or in your body, are reflections of emotional turmoil taking place. Either you have suppressed or repressed emotions that you could/should have brought up, and the water starts to go brown, brackish as the 'old' stuff regurgitates.

You might find leaks in the washing machine or the dishwasher, which are showing you that you are leaking emotion to something, some event or more likely a person. Either way, look to your emotional health when water starts to do unusual things in your house.
I remember when my husband, Bill, and I were living in our first house together. There was a lot of emotional turmoil around his ex wife's behaviour toward us. We had a pumped water

system at the time, from a deeply dug well. What fun we had, as the water went through all the ways it could have, reflecting back to us what was going on in our lives.

Sometimes, we had overflows. Sometimes, dark brown water, pump failure, shower not working, no water for days. Basically, a catalogue of different disasters that warrant a book on their own.
However, we did notice this phenomenon, and were able to look at things in a different way, because of the messages the water was bringing to us - and that was before the days of Emoto Massaru's books on water.

Current

As we have already discussed, we are all part of an electro magnetic field. Just as water has its way of showing up emotional situations, electricity has a way of highlighting when blockages in the energetic flow are occurring. When things fail, perhaps it is time to assess if you need a rest. Perhaps, whatever it is that has conked out, is delivering the message that you need to take time out. If a fuse has gone, then perhaps you need to look at your own fuses, to see if one has blown or not. It depends on what a fuse means to you. I know for me, I would say I had blown a fuse if I had become very angry about something. But, suppose you had blown a fuse and you hadn't expressed it, then the volatile emotion goes inward and takes its effect out on your inner fuse board and pop, something goes.

Blocks in the flow can surface as health problems and/or financial problems and/or present as entities that need clearing. You simply need to bring it into your awareness, and, of course, ask for Archangelic Guidance as to what you need to address.

If we are not expressing our innate ability to heal and channel energy that too can cause blocks in your flow, causing unusually hot flushes and or painful arms and hands. We all have this ability, and embracing it is the way forward to increasing the flow of energy and its current through your body.

Energetic dirt

The house can also be energetically dirty, that is to say everyone who lives in, and visits your house, brings their own energy imprint and that can be positive or negative. This energy hangs around. It delights in sticking in corners and around furniture. Also, remember the power of your words. If words have been shared in love - that is great, love will permeate the air. If, on the other hand, words of anger or dissent, swearing, anything with a negative connotation or spin, leave their energetic imprint, and can cover the place in wadges of lovely dark cloying energy.

Heartsound is at hand to deal with this. It is so easy to clear your house of all extraneous energy, simply by connecting to Heartsound,

Connect to your intention and focus, which is simply done by affirming.

Invocation and Affirmation

"I now Invoke the power and presence of the Archangels Michael and Gabriel and El Morya, the Ascended Master, I ask for your protection and assistance to clear my house or this room of any energies that are not of the Light."

"I am now cleansing and clearing this room (do one room at a time) of all, and any negative energy. Go to the light".

Make your Heartsound, AAhh, three or four times. You may need to go and stand in the corners of each room to sound out at least three times, until you feel a significant shift. Go around the entire house, and notice the difference. The clarity that will appear is astonishing and really noticeable.

Remember, 'As within so without, as without so within.'
As you clear your house, you also clear your inner house or temple, and rid yourself of old clingy negative energy.

Archangelic Assistance

Call on all the Archangels of Love and Light to help clear your house.

Archangel Michael will come in and show you what has to go. He will point it out with his sword, and you will see him cut away the ties that bind you to that old sofa you love so much, or your old toys or drums or whatever it is that you no longer need to burden you down in this lifetime.

Your ego will often come in to talk you out of letting go and detaching. For example, it will try to convince you that you might need that set of drums. Next week, when Phil Collins asks you to play a gig for him, or even wee Johnny down at the local pub might ask you to play in the bar. This can cloud your mind from the fact that, in the letting go, you allow the Universe its flowing ways. If necessary and if you need them, it will bring a set of drums back to you. However, it will be a better set than the ones you parted with.

The Universe will bring you whatever you need - when you need it. It will be bigger and better than anything you have every had before. The Universe is always listening, not just when you consciously address it. Be careful what you ask for – The Big Universe Is listening!

Material goods are not what are important. It is what and who you are, and who you are aspiring to be. Whatever you choose to sell or get rid of,(the unwanted, no longer useful or loved items) will raise your vibration another notch, until you are travelling so light, (weight as well) you will literally fly, find your wings, and use them to ascend and rise above everything, particularly the slavery that has been implanted in us.

Slavery to an excess of the material hedonistic life and all that brings with it. For example, the car, the house, what the neighbours might think, what your friends are doing or are not doing, holidays abroad. There is nothing wrong with a high standard of living. However, sustaining it when you are not in the flow is costly. It usually involves being in debt on your credit cards or with a huge mortgage.

The worry and anxiety that comes from debt, does not bring the 'peace that passeth all understanding' that flows from the heart. The heart of God that is within each and everyone of us. When we get our egos out of this scenario, then we can be free.

Instead it 'bringeth the pain in the backside', (polite version) and the pressure of having to earn more and more, to pay it all back with the interest.
People want to be financially free. I hear them talk of that every day. It allows them to make empowering choices, enjoy comforts and a high standard of living and help others in need.

If you are in debt, it is a constant leak of your energy. You give your power away to worry and anxiety, which can bring on a feeling of paralysis, and that nothing can be done. Only you can fix this. Do something about it. Choose to be financially free. Pay back the cards, cut them up. Keep one for booking flights and some of the items that can only be purchased on line.

Come up with ideas that will help you raise cash by selling off the stuff you no longer want on Ebay or a car boot sale/ garage sale. Use your entrepreneurial skills, have a brainstorming session with colleagues, family and friends come up with new ideas for your business or employ that could earn you more money.

We have all been given the gifts, talents and learned skills that will earn us an honest living. Start being innovative and think 'out of the box'. Start to think, and talk with Mother, Father God. They are the best 'brainstormers' of them all. You will be given brilliant ideas in meditation. Trust the answers that are given. As I realise I don't like the word 'brainstorming', as it has a kind of war like connotation, let's think of something more exciting like brainspiration. I like that. It encompasses more of what I am meaning.

Taking the first step out of the immobility feeling will make you feel really good. It will inspire you and, by putting love into all the little things you do every day, your work will become a joy. This, along with car and house clearing, will go a long way to cleansing, clearing and balancing your entire energy field.

Into the Oneness

I know that when we get our energy field healthy and vibrating at a high frequency, then we are totally in the ONENESS, without blocks, in the flow. And at that point, we can vibrate the web of life. We can co-create and manifest whatever we can think of, visualise and feel.

If that is not what is happening in your life, then you are still work in progress. That is OK. That is the way it is that is where most of us are. The purpose of this book is to help you work on the blocks, identify and clear them away. You will then notice a miraculous shift in the flow of your life, financial and otherwise.

Holistic freedom embraces so much more than just finances. All the things we have in this country, freedom of speech, freedom to be an activist for whatever cause you choose. Freedom to express your sexuality whatever way that is right for you. Independent of the negative opinion of other people in your life - your family and friends. Being your own person, freedom to be who you are, a child of this Universe, totally unique.

So few of us use our freedom of speech by playing small, not speaking up, not voting, because we think it is a waste of time. We think that what we have to contribute doesn't count. If that is what we collectively think, then we will be right. Let's choose to amend and change our attitude

Hopefully, after reading this book, you will feel inspired to get up, speak out, be the change you want to see. Lead by example and walk your talk.
Not - **do as I say -** but - **do as I do.**
Be a leader - and walk your talk.

I had feedback after a VIVA 1 workshop, when one of the participants phoned me to tell me that he wasn't sure what had happened. However, he was going through his house clearing cupboards at an amazing rate. He felt it was an odd thing to do, but said it felt powerful at the same time. It was almost as if it were happening to him rather than him controlling the impulse to do this. He felt lighter in every way.

This chap was a Reiki Master who had been practicing Reiki for a few years. Even so, using the Heartsound in a focussed and intentional way, had changed his life dramatically. On the day of the workshop he had chosen to let go of patterns that no longer served, and it had resulted in this mighty clear out. He was happily engaged in throwing out all the old, and clearing the way for the new to enter in.

Using the guided meditation below, we can connect deeply with the body, and talk with it about the excess of fat that we are carrying, find out the best way to shift, and also Heartsound to alter metabolism and eradicate addictions. Most people are not aware that the most common addiction we have is to sugar, and that puts on lots of weight, and can, of course, in time lead to more serious dysfunction of our beloved temple.

Normalising Your Weight

You can go on as many diets as you like, with varying degrees of success, however, unless you address the root causes of the excess weight, results will be temporary. When you return to your normal eating habits and routines, the weight will come back once again. The answer is a simple, yet effective one. You can choose to have a dialogue and a soundialogue with your body.

This is a free, one to one session with yourself. You are the leading expert on how your body is doing, what excess baggage it is carrying, and how to get rid of it. All the answers are available to you from your inner sage. Prepare in the usual way for meditation, take sacred space and relax. This will take about 20 minutes of uninterrupted time.

Meditation, creative visualisation and soundialogue.

Breathe, into the cello belly, pay particular attention to the exhale, and remember to exhale really slowly.

Allowing the muscles and joints to relax and let go,

Allowing the whole being to surrender to the peace and calm of your inner world, and the journey to the centre of your Universe, deep within.

As you allow your body to relax more and more you feel yourself becoming heavier, more and more connected to the chair or couch you are sitting in.

You feel warm. A wave of comfort spreads from head to toe, as you send loving thoughts to your body, reminding it how grateful you are to it for having carried you thus far on your journey.

As you check in to every area of your body, you switch a light on in each department.
Let's start with the head.

Take your awareness in there, and switch on a beautiful shimmering light.

As you do this, feel your brain relax.

Take your awareness to your throat, be aware of all the tensions there.

Allow it to relax, and switch the light on in there.

You will be aware of the strength of the light, as you feel it pulsating and penetrating every cell, every atom of your sub atomic cellular structure. You are being healed by these lights, so enjoy the process of switching them on.

Now, the lungs need a light switched on. Go ahead and do that, and feel the radiation of the light, as it expands into the cavities of your lungs.

We progress to your heart centre, and switch a light on in there. This joins the wonderful tri-fold light that is already present there. It amplifies and boosts this light, and there is a feeling of pink love floating through your heart space right now.

Proceed down the trunk of your body, taking time to switch lights on in all the major organs, including the liver, the spleen, the gall bladder, the digestive system, the reproductive system, colon and bowels. Keep going down your legs until you reach your feet, and fill the tips of your toes with light.

Allow five minute to do this.

Now, we are going to open the door to your heart centre. It opens wide in front of you, and you can see there is a passageway, taking you deep within yourself. It leads to a staircase of five steps that take you down to a lower floor and landing. You see ahead of you, a lift. Go in and select the ground floor button. As you press this, the doors close, and you feel the lift engaging, taking you down and down towards the ground floor.

You are now happily on the ground floor, focussing your inner concentration on the room ahead of you. You see a beautiful doorway, which you go through. This room is called the 'Balancing Room', a place where balance is restored by you to all aspects of your life. However, for the purposes of this visualisation, you are focussing on balancing your weight.

You ask Archangels Sandalphon and Raphael to be with you during this process. They are standing right beside you now. You acknowledge their presence, and they show you a glass three dimensional version of your body, with all the extra inches that are distributed here and there. They are also showing you a table loaded with all the things that you consume on an average week.

Raphael takes you by the hand, and is pointing out to you right now, the items that are not supportive to your weight balance. Items that are causing you to manufacture fat and store it. You have a pen and paper. Make a note of these, as he points them out. Raphael will even tell you which ones you can have a little of, which ones you should have more of, and what you are allowed as a treat. This could take a little while, don't try to rush this, it will take as long as it takes.

When you have noted everything down he will hand you over to Archangel Uriel, who has also joined you. He is showing you different exercises that you could be doing to help tone your body. This takes the form of a dance and beautiful music is being played. You find you can't help but move your body to this sound. You feel muscles stretching and you feel your lungs filling with oxygen, and expanding, as these beautiful movements seem to caress your body and it purrs with sensuous pleasure.

Archangel Sandalphon is now with you, making toning sounds into different parts of your body. You feel this unusual vibration, particularly in your spleen, where the weight balance issues live. He is encouraging you to send love to your spleen and send it sweet thoughts.

He encourages you to make the Heartsound of 'AAhh' along with him. Your focussed intention is to send sweet loving feelings into every organ in your body along with grateful thanks, particularly the bits that you regularly berate like your stomach and bottom, perhaps your breasts. You will know what it is for you, which parts you have hated, because now you are going to love them - big time, and restore them to their absolute glory.

The Archangels are guiding you to sit down. They are showing you a film of your lifetime, this life so far. It is on a huge screen, and is correct in every detail.

You notice the patterns that were playing out around you as you turned to food for comfort in your life, times when comfort wasn't forthcoming from anywhere else. Notice the dramas that were taking place. Allow Archangel Michael to help you detach from those scenes. See him removing the cords that may bind you to them in any way. As he takes all this to the Light, you will feel a lot lighter and liberated. He asks you now to forgive all the people involved, and most importantly yourself, as guilt is a useless energy to carry and it lowers your vibration.

Say out loud, "I forgive all those involved, and I forgive myself and set us all free."

Say that three times.

You may not feel that you totally mean it as yet, but the more you repeat it, the more it will become your Truth.

Give yourself a hug. In the film, you will see all the weights from these dramas being lifted from your shoulders by beautiful blue angels, as love and forgiveness come in, flooding everything and everyone.

You can see unconditional love as a beautiful pink shimmering colour. It is sweet and flows like honey. The blue angels ask you to say three times the following affirmation.

"I now choose to deeply and profoundly, accept, approve of, and love myself more and more each day."

The Archangels now ask you to take away all the information they have given you, and to listen to this, or do this visualisation every day – for fourteen days. Then, notice how you feel about yourself. How much trimmer you are, and how much better you feel about yourself in every way. Balance is being fully restored.

Affirmation.

"I now choose to take back my power. To exert the willpower required. To rebalance my weight by eating and drinking only the foods and beverages in correct quantity that are truly supportive to my well being."

Thank the Archangels, and see them drift away.

Now you are going to come back up the lift.
Coming back gently and slowly into the present moment.

When you are ready, open your eyes and reconnect with this amazing Universe.

How do you feel? What was the list that you were given.

Write everything down, knowing that you are being supported in this endeavour by the Higher Realms and the Archangels of Love and Light.

Expanding Heartsound

Heart-sound to improve your singing, inspire your presenting and magnetise your manifesting.

When clients come to me for voice coaching, their concerns are usually about breathing, volume, tone, sustaining, lack of confidence and self-esteem. As you have seen from earlier chapters, they are all connected. There can be a lot going on in the subconscious mind that is affecting the conscious performance. Having dealt with the subconscious issues, let's take a look at the basic functions.

Here are some tips on how to harness the power of your voice, so that it sounds the way you would like it to sound, by using Heartsound as your basic recipe. Also, further information on how to deliver your message with ease and self-confidence. This will rid you of self-consciousness, blushing, palpitations, panic attacks, bowel problems and sweating, to name but a few delightful symptoms of performance fear.

Awareness of 'shouldering'

I have already shared the 'cello belly' way of breathing with you. In addition to that, I would like you to become more aware of yourself as you breathe.

Use a mirror, stand in front of it, and begin to breathe in from the pubic bone - in - and then release. As you watch yourself, watch for your shoulders moving. They shouldn't move at all if you are breathing correctly. Also, put your hands around your rib cage and breathe in and out. Feel your hands moving in and out with the breath. Your shoulders are not involved. However, your lower lungs, your diaphragm and your cello belly are very much involved.
Practice this- and practice it a lot.

If you use your shoulders a lot when you breathe, it is likely that you take on a lot of responsibility. Do you need to? Is it your responsiblity? Think about it.

Heart-sound for stamina and sustaining.

Move on to practice making Heartsound - the sound of 'AAHH' - for as long as you can hold the note. The more you do this, the longer you will be able to hold, as your lungs respond to being used properly and expand accordingly.

You will begin to feel a response deep within you. This is the place where you know you can go to hold the note steadily yet in a relaxed way. If you hear your voice vibrating and oscillating between two notes, then you are trying too hard, and at some level, trying to control your sound from the throat. (Otherwise known as heavy vibrato).

Bypass your throat, and open out. Allow the sound to reach your belly button, allow it to drop naturally. Let go of control.

Singing exercises and melody

Using scales, various little tunes and arpeggios are great for stretching your voice. A bit like Yoga for the voice, and practice makes perfect. Like any musical instrument, your voice responds to being used and used often. Never worry that you are hurting your throat. It is simple, if pain starts up, then you are hurting it. Stop what you are doing immediately and rest. Fifteen minutes vocal exercise every day is sufficient to begin with to build up strength and flexibility.

Presentation

In previous chapters, we have looked at ways of ridding yourself of low self-esteem and low self-confidence, so I won't repeat that here. However, one of the best tips, whether singing in a concert or talking at an event, is to send love out to the audience prior to your appearance. I always use pink

bubbles of unconditional love, and see them landing on people and bursting over their heads, showering them with love and light.
I often tune in days before, and send VIVA energy through to the performance in advance.

Remember time is simply energy, and you can tune in to the past or the future. Sending positive vibrations into the whole performance, raises the energy of the event, and carries you through in peace and calm.

The Angels of Love will carry the love forward to each and every member of the audience. They only need to hear one word from you that could change their life forever. Just one word, just one note from a song, just one phrase from the lyric.

Isn't that amazing, such is the power of the voice, the word and the song.

The only thing that will hold you back is your ego, and you now know how to deal with that. Take control, dialogue, encourage it to 'Bless Off' for a well earned rest. It simply speaks with forked tongue, and it is not the Truth. You now know that, or you may need to read through parts of this book again!

You are unique, nobody does it quite like you. You are the man or the woman! Do it and bring JOY and LOVE to it. If that doesn't happen, maybe you need to really assess and re-evaluate. Is this what really makes your Heart Sing? Check in by asking your Heart.

Question

"Hello Heart, am I really following the correct career/ life path for me?"

Now listen to the reply. Either, you will feel really comfortable, in which case, that would be a 'YES'. On the other hand, if you feel in any way discomfited, any slight gnawing feelings, distortion of any kind in the gut area, then you need to ask more questions to tease out the answer.

Learning to trust these reactions is really all about getting to know yourself, I am still polishing that skill, however, I find the more I trust, the easier it becomes, or should I say, the replies seem more obvious.

Be aware of when EGO comes in. Ego makes decisions and judgements from fear based information, conscious or not. The Divine human that you are, makes decisions based on love, and the inner knowledge that you and the Divine Source of All That Is, are One. So, whatever happens, and that could include the audience throwing rotten tomatoes at you, it would all be in Divine Right Order, it is all meant to be, and that is the way it is.

In the sure knowledge that you are working for a much higher vibration and serving the Light, you will always be protected, and you are strong enough to withstand 'the slings and arrows' with the help of the Legions of Light.

As you rise above the EGO, you understand more of what your mission is on this planet - at this time, as you allow yourself to be spoken or soul sung or sounded. In other words, GET OUT OF YOUR OWN WAY. Allow the Higher realms to take the strain. They surely will. It is about knowing that they will never let you down. They are there to speak the Truth through you, and this is exactly what happens.

When you employ all of that, 'failure' simply isn't a word that you could use alongside Divinely guided words. it just isn't an option, because it would simply be a judgement.

This hopefully will have helped you in looking at performing or presenting in a totally different way. It is not about you, it is about the message of the song, the melody or the words, the speech. The audience have chosen to be there to hear that message. Enjoy being the Messenger, and detach from the outcome of what you are doing and saying. Let them have their own experience. As long as what you are saying or performing has integrity. And it will, if it comes from your Heart, your place of Truth, all will be very well.

Manifesting with Music and Heartsound

Using the Heartsound technique, you can manifest whatever you want in your life.

Make your list of Heart's Desires, as many as you like.

Focus on one each day for the next twenty one days. During this time, you will repeat some, and that is fine. Just keep going back to the beginning of the list.

Soundisation

Take sacred space.

Play music in the back ground that you enjoy, music that you find inspiring, or choose to be in silence. The sound of silence has much to offer too. Whatever floats your boat, do it.

Take your awareness to your heart, and as per previous instructions, connect to your Heart-sound.

Begin making the sound of 'AAHH'. At the same time, put your undivided attention and focussed intention on to your heart's desire.

Always put in the rider that, if this is for your Highest Good, and the Highest good of all concerned, then you will certainly magnetise and manifest this desire to yourself, from the web of life.

Just KNOW that, as you send your transmission out onto the web of life, it is being received by the power of the Universe.

It is co-creating this reality with you right now. Divine Right Timing is also in play. Your desires will arrive when the time is right - and not before.

Whatever you want already exists, even as you thought of it, and it's on its way, so now move into a place of heartfelt gratitude for the delivery of your co-creation.

See it arriving. Feel how you will feel on the day it arrives, and keep sounding your Heart-sound with joy, as you welcome your heart's desire into your energetic field of consciousness.

It is done. Keep sounding with love and joy until you feel your energy shifting, then bring yourself back to the room.

Well done, you are now a manifester and magnetiser. Tomorrow you can start on the next item on your list of forthcoming Heart's Desires.

Be Specific

I cannot encourage you enough to be absolutely specific about what you want.
Recently I received the message that it is time to move to a different location. I discussed this strong feeling with my husband. To my surprise, Bill said that he wasn't surprised at all, it seemed like the right time to move on. We contacted the estate agents and organised putting the house on the market.

As soon as we had done that, a friend visited, and, while she was with us, I was prompted by the Archangels to suggest to her that she should buy a house in town, seek a change of use, and turn it in to a healing centre, with a GP as well as herself, a homeopathic practitioner. As an after thought, I added that Bill and I could possibly help out too, as therapists.

She thought this to be a great idea and being a woman of integrity and financial means, she would be able to fund this project and the thought of us acting as Manager/ Caretakers was also on the table for discussion. It all seemed to fit. The Universe had come up with the complete package, including a new house to live in.

Now then, this was a goal, a dream, that has somehow always burbled around in the background of my mind and part of me was over the moon with excitement. Another part of me thought, no way, this doesn't feel quite right. I was being presented with the manifestation to one of my desires on a plate.

It took me back to my name and the definition of IRIS. If you remember, it is all about self-empowerment. My habitual pattern in life has been to get involved in other people's projects, invest enormous amounts of energy in them, and really not doing what I am meant to be doing. I have to say, writing this book would be an example of what I am meant to be doing.

With this realisation, I immediately checked in to the Higher Consciousness in meditation, and with divination, using my dowsing crystal. The crystallisation of clarity dawned. I was simply the messenger for my friend. She was the one to action the plan. I could also put her in touch with GPs in the Highlands who are also therapists I have trained in Reiki as well.

At some level, I could help her to manifest her dreams. I realised with great clarity that I had been presented with this dream realisation as a test. I was equally clear that I didn't want it for me at this time. I didn't want to be stuck in a clinic. The Archangels have made it clear that they need me to put myself 'out there', and do what I do best, and that is, speak about all this kind of metaphysical wonder with audiences across the globe. I am affirming that invitations of integrity to do this will begin to appear.

I didn't get sucked in to this scenario, so I am pleased about that. I am sharing the story with you to illustrate the point about being specific, and to check out what you are manifesting for.

Is it really the right thing for you?
Will it make your heart sing?
Is it in alignment with your soul purpose?

It is also about noticing the things that you are not *consciously* manifesting, ideas lurking in the back of your mind!

I would like to share a really solid way of coming up with the answers you need to know for yourself. Pendulum crystal dowsing really works for me, I have utmost faith in my little pointed pink rose quartz crystal. It needs to be treated with respect, and it is best to go into a sacred space to use it. You can buy them in most Mind, Body and Spirit Shops.

How to use your crystal.

First of all, address your pendulum. Welcome it into your life. Cleanse and clear it of all old programmes, by making Heart-sound into it, until you feel its energy shift, holding that intention in your mind.

Now re-programme it. Ask it kindly to meld and merge with your Higher Consciousness, and whatever is for your well being and highest good.

Make Heart-sound again to seal this new programme in.

Thank this beautiful pendulum for being in your life and bless it.

Ask the Archangel Michael to bless it for you.

Next, hold the pendulum in your dominant hand by its chain, so that the crystal itself is free to swing. Ask it to show you what a 'YES' would look like. It will begin to swing from, east to west or west to east , or from north to south or south to north.

You will feel the pull. Keep doing it until you do feel the pull. Log the direction it gives you. That is your YES.

Then, ask it to show you what NO is and again it will swing, usually in the opposite direction, it will be distinct from the YES movement.

It is different for everyone, so don't compare. You are unique, and your crystal is working and merging with you, as it has become part of your vibrational field.

Now we come to the tricky part. You need to frame your questions in such a way that only 'Yes' or 'No' can be the answers. Obviously, the crystal cannot give you more than that. It is an exercise in framing questions well.

I'll give you good examples.
Q. "Do you feel that I should move to a new location?"

Yes or No?

Q. "Do you feel that London would be a good move for me?"

Yes or No?

Q. "Would Glasgow be a better choice for me?"

Yes or No?

Q. "Would South/North/ West/ East of Glasgow be best?"

Yes or No?

Keep going until you have pinned it down. You can refine and refine questions until the answers become very clear. Trusting and having faith are all part of this, and your crystal is listening to every word you say, so treat it with respect.

These kind of questions help you to tap into the 'THY WILL and not MY WILL' ethos, which is so important when you become an instrument and servant of the Divine. It helps to be doing what Higher Consciousness wants you to be doing, and not off on your own little ploys - lovely though they are. They tend to be detours, where you get enormous lessons before you decide to get back on track. Lessons are always good, however, a more peaceful existence (not necessarily lesson free) is awaiting you when you stay on track.

You will also find that the more you do this, the more often you will hear the 'Yes' or 'NO', even before your pendulum starts to move. That is really validating. There will also come a time when you can set the crystal aside, and listen and trust the answer that comes in as being the Truth.

So do check in for this strong guidance. I am writing this for me as well as you. I often need to remind myself of this one.

Practice this now, use a piece of jewellery if you don't have a crystal dowser as yet. Take time to write down the answers.

Oneness

I AM
I am love
I am love in action
I am love in action right now
Every minute of every day
Every word, everything I say
I am here to heal and pray
I am here to show the way

Who are you?
Who can you be?
Is your heart open to see?
Is your heart open to Me
Walk with Me, talk with Me
I am you, you are Me
You are my eyes to see
My voice, my way to be

You are
You are love
We are
We are love
We are love in action right now
We are joy and fulfilment
We are the source of creation
Together the Divine instrument

We are the Oneness.

Patricia Iris July 2007

Power of Prayer

This book is about the power of the spoken word and the sound of the voice. When we stand in the power of who we truly are, using our full body voice, and speaking or performing from the heart, then, when we merge together in the Oneness. We can shift mountains, build pyramids, change attitudes and change paradigm beliefs.

I am not religious, yet, I salute the organised religions who use the power of prayer in their various traditions, appealing for help from a beneficent God, somewhere up there or out there. I accept and respect their beliefs, for that is their teaching and understanding, passed down to them from their ancestors.

For me, although born into a Protestant family in Glasgow, Scotland, I choose very consciously to go within, and merge with the Source within me. I go within to vibrate the web of Truth, the web of Divine Humanity. I do this in the sure knowledge that the entire Hierarchy of Vibration, which is the Light with which I am aligned, attuned and merged with, is part of our web.

In that Oneness, the Source of All that Is, responds to our every prayer and Heart call. Judgement is non-existent in that field of consciousness. There is no good or evil. There is just simply 'what is'. People engaged in their own Divine Drama, which will take them nearer to their ascension, should they choose to wake up and live the journey consciously.

As we have prayed for peace in our world, the worst sores of anger and repression have raised up. They have been stifled for millennia, and now they strike out with hatred in their hearts. However, we need to be mindful that this understandable reaction is the healing in itself.

As the grievance and the hatred are brought to the surface, so the Unconditional Love emanating from the Oneness, will heal and console it. Gently reminding it - that we are all one.

You are my brother and sister, you and I are One. We are all different aspects of the Oneness. Respecting this, remembering this, helps us to understand with grace and love, what is happening on our planet right now.

We have choices. Do we choose to feed the monster within and without - called fear?

Do we choose to energise and expand it, or do we choose to have Faith and Trust that Love will prevail? As the Light has already won, there is, in reality, no contest. However, we need to constantly reaffirm our Love, Faith, Trust and Gratitude, in order to keep it nourished, alive and kicking within us.

Descending back into fear would be the fall back place of the old paradigm belief. However, as we move forward into our ascension time with Mother Earth we know that all is in Divine Right Order. That out of this chaos, peace will emerge as long as we remain steadfast on **focussing on the peace**.

Let us pray together for Peace, by using our Divine VIVA VOCE - the Living Voice – by using our entire presence to communicate our feelings and thoughts to the web of life, and all therein.

Read this prayer out loud. Let Divine Intelligence hear every word.

"Source of All That Is, within me, I acknowledge and welcome your presence deep within my every cell. I am filled with love, respect, honour and gratitude for your existence and Oneness with me. I listen eagerly in the Silence for your every word of guidance. I lift my voice to speak the words you prompt me to say and express. With your wisdom, I find the compassion and forgiveness within my Soul, to forgive, not only myself, but Divine Humanity for anything and everything that they do and have done, that is not of the Light. Thank you for healing humanity's pain and anguish, the anger and hatred. Thank you for bringing it out into the open so that it can be healed and transmuted to the Light with love.

I am redefining my spiritual life infusing it with joy and love. With your love and support, I am releasing judgement and fear, accepting what is, and entering in to a new relationship with you, myself and Humanity. I now choose to recognise, celebrate and be the Oneness.

I thank you for the Peace that is pouring into our lives. Into each and every heart, each and every village and town, each and every country and continent, until it pervades the entire planet.

All of the kingdoms of this Earth are rejoicing and harmonising, as we make our Heart-sound of 'AAHH'. We sound it out loud and clear, heralding the arrival of the songs and sounds of the new vibrations and dimensions.

Love for All by All.
Peace within and without,
Peace for All.

The Power of Blessings.

When you apply mindfulness and awareness to your life, you begin to notice the small things, the minutiae of life.

Just the other day, a little white mouse came in to my potting shed, where I have written a lot of this book. It played around, and then tried very hard to leverage itself up into a planter in search of something, who knows what. The little thing was disturbed by Brook, my brother's dog, and off it scampered. It left me wondering why it had scampered in to my life, as I have not seen a mouse in and around the garden before.

In shamanic terms, mouse medicine means details, and paying attention to them. I took it as a sign to remember to mention awareness. Being in the present moment, and loving and blessing everything we do, and everyone with whom we share our lives. As we do this, we imbue everything with unconditional Love and Gratitude, two of the most powerful emotions that we can ever express. They immediately connect us to our hearts, and to the Source, opening our hearts out into expansive states of bliss.

Blessing someone, something or anything, immediately raises the vibration of the one in receipt of your good intentions. It seems like a powerful recipe for both the giver and the receiver, which is what abundance is. Giving and receiving in balanced flow, without distortion of any kind, whether in relationship, in financial terms or with our energy.

Being a bridge between the place of infinite blessings and unconditional love with humanity, is a Love-workers role, and one which, if embarked upon, fulfils your role of service, at the simplest of levels.

Make it your goal today and every day, to bless as many people, places, animals, situations, food, water, possessions as you can possibly dream up. Pour your unconditional love into life from the largest of pouring jugs you can imagine, without expectation, and simply notice how that unconditional love returns to you ten fold.

It is easy to be loving and kind to those around us that are loving and kind. There are also those around us that challenge us. They don't behave in a way we expect them to, or in a way that matches our standards. When we separate the behaviour from the individual, we are left with an individual spirit, doing the best they can, with the knowledge that they have. Our job is to learn to forgive, love and bless the spirit, not condone the poor behaviour - just acknowledge that it is their behaviour.

Standing in our own power, and not giving it away to the drama or the behaviour, means that we are loving, honouring and respecting ourselves. This comes from a place of high self-esteem. The next time a situation occurs where it would be a possibility for you to enter into a lively dialogue, simply acknowledge, pull back, bless the situation and honour yourself by saving your energy and power, and not feeding the individual or the drama with your power. Instead, turn your thoughts again to blessing. How could you bless the individual causing the discord?

How many ways could you bless people as you walk down the street for example?

Write them down.

As you sit in a train or on a bus or even in your car, how many ways could you bless those around you?

Write them down.

Silently bless, bless with Heart- sound. Tune into the sound of the train, or the bus or car. Merge your sound with it, and send the sound out through the pink ribbon of connection, sound your silent blessings.

Remember also to bless yourself every day, as you are a blessing on this planet at this time, much loved and much appreciated for all the work you are doing on yourself and humanity.

Be open to receiving wonderful blessings of love and joy. Throw your arms open to embrace these blessings, as they flow to you from the infinite fountain of blessings in the Universe.

Every morning, throw your arms open and invite the Illumined Beings of Light to fill your entire being with wondrous positivity and a wealth of love, as the day unfolds in Divine Right Order.

Positivity opens the doorways to an abundance of love and joy in your life.

Affirmation

"I am open to receive the blessings of Love, Light and Joy from the Illumined Beings of Light"

Say this many times during the day, and feel your vibration lift, as you entrain with the energy of the Higher Consciousness.

Take a moment to write down how you will change your morning routine to accommodate prayer, blessings, these new affirmations and ways of being.

The shower is a wonderful sound dome that you can use as your place of connection to Heart sound and set the right tone for the day!

Divine Intelligence is listening for your early morning song!

Connection to the Oneness with Heartsound

We have the ability to connect to anything and everything, as we are all part of the one. Therefore, if, for example, you wish to actively connect with a flower essence or a colour, a book, the elements or a particular person - or even a particular Illumined Being, all you need to do is a Heartsound with Activated Connection.

As an example, this evening I am going to be in the company of Mother Meera, and have Darshan, which is her blessing. She is a being of pure love, and one of the highest Avatars of Light on the planet at this moment.

During my morning meditation and Heart-sound practice, I decided to tune in to Mother Meera. I had already done this during the week, and was aware that Mother Meera was already working with me in spirit, or dancing with me in Spirit - as I prefer to say. I tuned in by sending my Heart-sound out in a beautiful pink ribbon towards her heart. I could see her clearly in my mind's eye, although we have never met. The ribbon connected to her heart, and I felt a most beautiful soft pink energy merge with mine. It came all the way back along the connecting ribbon, and pervaded my whole being. I was then told to come and write this section of the book, as you need to know how to do this simple, yet effective technique, and explore ways that you can use it to accelerate your healing and ascension.

Think of the wonderful and inspiring people you could choose to connect to, ask for their personal help and motivation. Wouldn't that be such a blessing?

To be in integrity, I feel we should always ask for permission. In the case of Mother Meera, this is her 'raison d'etre', her reason for being on the planet. However, I simply wouldn't want to enter someone's energy field if they were not happy with that. It is best to honour others, as indeed, you would want to be honoured yourself.

The Illumined beings are also there to help us, and they are used to us invoking their presence, as we have already done in this book. This is another way to simply merge with them. It has profound results, so take five minutes right now and give it a try.

Visualisation and Soundisation

Take sacred space, take your awareness to your breathing, focus on the out breath.
Take your awareness to your heart centre, and breathe into it, as you walk into the secret chamber, and stand beside your tri-fold flame.

Walk through the flame, allow it to cleanse you completely, and descend down the steps to the lower landing, where you can walk into your inner cathedral.

Sit down and tune in to your heart, feel the qualities of loving wisdom within your heart, and make your beautiful, unique and authentic Heart-sound.

With this underway, take your awareness to your heart, and see the pink ribbon of unconditional love unfold from it.

Send it out to the Illumined Being that you have decided to connect with today, and notice how you feel as your ribbon merges into that being.

See their heart open to receive your loving ribbon, and then allow the reciprocal movement and transaction to take place.

Feel the connection, feel the attributes and powers of this Being merge with your whole body system.

Absorb the energy, be like a sponge.

Dwell in it, allow it to lift you higher in your vibration, allow all to fall away that is not congruent with this level of light. Send lots of loving thoughts of gratitude, and withdraw when it feels right.

Gently and assuredly come back up the steps to your secret chamber, acknowledge how your Light has grown, and become more illumined.

Lock the door of your secret chamber as you very gradually come back into consciousness in the room.

Welcome back to the wonderful Universe around you. How joyous and glorious was that??

Flower essences

I love vibrational flower essences, and I become so absorbed in reading about them. Sometimes I buy them, and sometimes I tune in with my Heart-sound and pink ribbon to their qualities, and absorb them in to my being. You can, of course, go straight to the plants and flowers themselves, and make the connection, and drink in the blissful cup of love that they offer us. Take time to make your heart connection. It doesn't need to take long. Simply centring and grounding, and then following the procedure above with focussed intention only takes minutes. Breathe the essence of the flower in, be with it, love it and be grateful for all the wondrous new energy that enters into your being.

Colour

Colour is so powerful. Intuitively you will reach for the colour that is right for you to wear every day of your life. Colours hold vibrant energy within their field that resonates with your field of consciousness, your chakras and your Aura. When you tune in to colours, and explore the deep insights that they can bring you, it opens a whole new world to you of self-discovery and a way of tapping in to your inner wisdom that is extremely powerful.

When you self-diagnose, (notice which colour you are drawn to for the day), and come up with the colour that is needed by your body, then you can connect with the essence of that colour by using the Heart-sound Activation Connection route.

Begin to make Heart-sound, and actively bring the qualities of that colour into your being. Your focussed intention will bring the field of colour into you. The sound being the conduit, that will meld and merge it with your entire being, with those millions of cells.

For example, there are times when I feel I need more passion in and about my life. I take sacred space, tune in to a deep passionate red colour and make Heart-sound. I sound passionate red. I go with, and Trust in, the sound that I have been given as passionate red! I take my awareness to my cellular structure, and fill every cell with the sound of this colour. I fill every chakra, and see them spin with the new colour. I transmute darkness with the sound of the new colour. I feel it lift and energise my vibration and increase my Light.

I begin to wear more and more of the colour that I need in my life. This is a huge subject. Using sound with colour is an evolutionary field that I urge you to investigate for yourself. Explore and enjoy!

Keeping it simple.

I feel that the pink ribbon is simple and easy to use, for everyone. We are all able to channel energy, so when you tune in to a friend or family member, and gain permission to work with them. This is done by simply asking the question, may I work with you? You will feel the answer and know whether it is right to proceed or not. If it's a YES you can send healing loving energy to them, for their highest good and the highest good of all concerned, to arrive at a time that is suitable for them. Remember, time is energy too, and you can bridge time by planning well in advance. I quite often use a pink bubble of loving healing light as well. I let it burst over their heads and shower the person with a warm comforting love.

I advised one of my Reiki student's in Glasgow to send pink bubbles to a colleague of hers who had a very low opinion of Reiki. She tended to make my student's life uncomfortable about it, to say the least. After about a year of pink bubbles and love and Light being sent to her, the same lady, who had been a thorn in my student's side, actually asked her for a session of Reiki, and became a regular client. So, pink works, Love and Light works. Just send lots of it out there! Now you can use this new method (HAC) and Heartsound it, Activate and Connect with Pink Ribbon of heart to heart connection.

Books

I was invited to work with a group of 6th year pupils at Fortrose Academy many years ago now. They were all involved in the Young Enterprise of the Year awards. Their teacher asked me to work with their confidence, self-esteem and self-belief. I used visualisation, guiding them into a deep space, where they accessed their own inner library, and received the answers to all the questions they had for their exams. Then, we did self-esteem boosting exercises. This was pre my Heartsound days, now I would use sound as well however even as it was, it was extremely successful.

I spoke to one of the pupils at the end of the session. He was the Dux (the guy with top marks, first in his year) of the school. I asked him if he had enjoyed the session, and he replied that he had, but he also said, "that is what I always do, I have done that since I was a child".

The rest of the group were stunned by this, and I could see the cogs going round in their minds, as lights went on all over the place!

Powerful stuff! So, now you can go to that place, and make Heartsound, to really cement the answers into your mind for your exams!

When we use Heartsound with focussed intention, we can do anything. We can use it in any context. However, it is about being mindful, and taking time to make a strong heart connection with the sound from the outset.

Medicine Woman and Swan Spirit

I decided last year to test out this theory. The theory being - to tune into, and connect with a subject, and then make Heart sound, whatever came in, not necessarily or exclusively the sound of AAHH. I shared the experiment with my good friend and fine musician, John Sinclair, who plays keyboard and is always game for exploring new things.

The first subject was Medicine Woman. John and I tuned in to each other, and then the subject. I tuned in to my Heartsound. A chord was played, and off we went. We recorded as we played. The CD at the back of the book, has the original recording, just as it all came out at the time.

I have received a lot of positive feedback from this music, from different people all over the world. Only one person didn't get a lot from it.

People have found it to be deeply emotional, profoundly healing and uplifting. Please email and let me know how you experienced it.

It has a profound effect on those who take sacred space and tune in, and really go with the sounds and the resonance.

Swan Spirit

I love swans and their graceful movements. My mother was a professional cellist and her favourite piece was The Swan, by Sans Saens, I love it too.

I had been on holiday on the islands of Orkney in March 2006. Near the Ring of Brogdar, a ring of ancient standing stones, there is a loch. When Bill and I visited, there were literally hundreds of swans feeding there. It was such a beautiful gift for our eyes and we were mesmerised for a long time, simply watching.

I spoke about this to Steven Farmer on my radio show. Steven is a shaman, (Doreen Virtue's husband), and very much into animal medicine, as am I. He told me that he felt the message from this scene was that, "you are held in a state of grace". As he said that I felt my vibration shift and go through the roof, as I usually do when a Truth is spoken. I thanked him and the Powers that be for delivering that wonderful message to me.

When John and I tuned in to 'Swan Spirit', I tuned in to that day, and the beautiful sight I had seen and the words that Steven had spoken. The track you hear on the recording is just as we recorded it at the time. People have listened, some have identified with Swan. Some however, have not. They have connected with healing and the resonance of the waves of sound. My radio producer thought that it should be put out on wider release. I am gifting this grace to you on the CD at the back of the book. Enjoy.

Remember 'Swan'. Remember to glide through life seamlessly, although you may be paddling fairly rapidly just beneath the water's surface. Stand in the power of your beauty, grace and peace.

I would love to have a huge choir assembled in Glasgow to make Heart-sound using our authentic voices for Peace.

Heartsound for Peace, I am going to take time to energise and manifest that one.

Take time to write down how you experience the music. Where does it take you - and how do you feel as you listen?

Viva Voce – The Living Voice

Viva Voce – Long live the voice

Well here we are at the final act, the conclusion of the story, the last chapter.

Yet, I feel that your journey with the conscious use of your voice is only just beginning. The Archangels Michael and Gabriel urge you to use the tools offered here to change and enrich your life. They won't do any good at all, if you don't actually use them. So, the thrust of this last gasp is to underline that fact.

Use your voice.

Affirmation

"I am using my voice every day, in co-creation with the Divine. I allow the will of the Divine to guide me as to how to use it for the service of humanity and our beautiful planet and the Universe."

Speak up
Speak out
Sing out
Sound out
With joy with happiness with love
With integrity and acceptance respect and honour
Let the Universe hear every word clearly.
Use your voice to uplift the Collective Vibration, lifting it ever higher.

Use your voice:
To give praise and encouragement
To appreciate each other
To send love

To heal your body
To harmonise humanity
To speak kindness
To remove fear
To open minds
To close old doors
To promote
To bless
To cherish moments
To sing for the world
To focus on what you are 'for' in life
To motivate others
To inspire and serve
To lift your spirit
To lift other's spirits
To be the voice of the 21st century
To re-empower the Divine Feminine in you and your fellow humans
To fill the room or the stage
To vibrate and resonate with Light
To send Light out into the world
Use your Divine Voice

Be the Divine Human Being you are capable of being.

Statement of Intent

Take space in your sacred room, where you know you won't be disturbed or overheard for about 10 minutes.

Place a piece of A4 card board or paper on the floor in front of you

Align yourself to the Universe and Mother Earth, calm yourself with your breath, put your roots down deep into the earth and make sure you are well grounded and rooted. At the same time be aware of your magical connection with Spirit.

Now speak out loud with conviction,

"I am choosing, in this moment right now, to stand in the power of my unique self and unique voice. I am a Divine Human Being, in service to the Hierarchy of Heaven. I am protected and loved, and await Thy guidance. Use me".

Now, step positively and meaningfully onto the white card. How does it feel, notice the feelings. This step signifies the powerful transformation you have taken. This is the place of the new you. How are you vibrating now?

Imagine the white card or paper spreading out all over the floor, so that everywhere you walk now, you are walking the new paradigms of love, light and blessing. The old paradigms of judgement, criticism and blame or playing small, are no longer part of your life or your script.

Congratulations

The Archangels of love and light thank you for the diligent work you have completed, and they look forward to working with you on your sacred path.
Give yourself a hug and lots of appreciation. Perhaps treat yourself to something you really love, as a 'well done' from Spirit - with whom you are One.

With Infinite Love and Blessings

Patricia Iris

Accompanying CD.

I have recorded some of the Meditations and Visualisations on the CD at the back for your convenience. I hope you enjoy. The remainder are available on another CD in my web shop.

Keeping up to date.

For newsletters and news of VIVA workshops near you, updates from the Illumined Beings of Love and Light and free downloads, please visit my web site www.patriciairis.com and register on the database.

Please tune in and listen to the 'Spiritual Matters' programme that I present on www.internetradio.co.uk, Inspiring interviews are available to download.

Please note that 10% of the income from this book is being donated to the Dandelion Trust specifically to help Madge Bray to re-introduce the Batonebe healing songs of Georgia to the Georgians, and the rest of the world. Further donations for this work are most welcome.

Thank you

Thank you to Spirit from the deepest part of my being, and to the beloved Archangels of Love and Light, and all Illumined Beings who have inspired this book - and its messages.

A huge 'Thank You' to my husband, Bill Kerins, for his patience in editing my work, and his loving support, which does include breakfast in bed.
Editors note: - very often!

Thanks also to Jamie Wonnacott, for his design and production.

Many thanks for the front cover to John Claudius, for his inspired painting of Archangel Michael, with his rainbow wings.

Deep gratitude also to John Sinclair for the beauty of his music in Medicine Woman and Swan Spirit.

There are many beautiful beings and friends of Light who have encouraged and supported my well being throughout this project. A sincere thanks to all.

A huge thanks to Wayne Dyer, for his wonderfully inspiring voice, and to Louise Love Hay and Maureen Moss, both powerful women of integrity, who have helped me enormously in my life's journey.

John Claudius

Artist John Claudius, born in India, where his father was a serving Police Officer until the final days of the Raj, now resides near Inverness, the Highland capital of Scotland.

His paintings, generally mixed media, have been inspired not only by the beautiful surrounding scenery, but also by many years involvement in Theatre as Director, Actor and Set designer, from London to Inverness.

John Sinclair

Based in the Highlands of Scotland, John is an ex rock band keyboard player who is now devoting his life to motivating youngsters through music, to achieving their full potential. He is co-creating the musical 'The Awakening' with Patricia Iris, and has worked with her on several musical projects.

Workshops.

Patricia Iris presents VIVA Levels 1 & 2 and Masters.

VIVA Level 1 Introductory

An opportunity to clear the karmic and ancestral patterns that block you from achieving your full potential. You will learn how to create a sound dome, use Heartsound for yourself and others.
You will receive an attunement to Archangelic Energy channelled by Patricia Iris.
Level 1 is a certificated course with workbook and CD. This level can be repeated as often as you feel it is necessary. (One day Workshop)

VIVA Level 2 Practitioner

Building on the knowledge gained at Level 1 you will learn how to balance chakras with Heartsound. Activate the axiatonal lines around the four body system. Working with the core star you will align your entire body with Heartsound clearing all segments of any distortions to your vibration and transmission. You will receive a further attunement to Archangelic Energy. You will feel confident to integrate Heartsound in to your existing therapy practice. (Two day workshop)

VIVA Master/ Teacher

Final attunement to re-empowering the Divine Feminine and bringing in the balance with the Divine Masculine..
You will be introduced to the whole teaching system of VIVA and how to channel the attunements as well as receiving the attunement to Source energy. You will spend a week in Heartsounding, meditation, realignment, cleansing, clearing and balancing. All stories and, false identities will be ditched, all the lights to switch on your true authentic self will be

activated in preparation for stepping in to this powerful role as Divine Human Being, Guide and Healer in service to Humanity and Mother Earth. This done you will be shown how to sustain this shift in your vibration. (One week retreat)

For current dates and venues please view:
www.patriciairis.com

VIVA Healing Sessions.

One to one sessions, restoring the Divine Feminine Power, are available over the telephone or face to face. To book an appointment please contact Patricia's office on:

+44 (0) 1250 871147

Useful Information

Harebell Remedies
81 Main St
St John's Town of Dalry
Castle Douglas
Dumfries and Galloway
DF7 3UP
Scotland.

Email ellie@harebellremedies.co.uk
Tel +44 (0) 1644 430 607

The Loving Harmony Initiative
The Dandelion Trust
41, The Limehouse Cut
46, Morris Rd
London E14 6NQ

Tel +44 (0) 20 7538 5633

www.dandeliontrust.org
Registered Charity No. 328159 Est.1988

Patricias Webshop.

Affirmation bookmarks

1. Archangel Michael

'I am a powerful spiritual warrior, working with Archangel Michael and the Legions of Light, to heal humanity..........Use Me'

2. Archangel Gabriel

'I am an inspirational instrument of Thy Divine Voice....Use Me'

Crystal Pendants for Dowsing

(A mixture of crystals and sizes)

Harebell Flower Remedies. (Extracted from their handbook).

Iris (Germanica)

Keywords; Power, Creativity, Expression.
The bold Iris reminds you of your best potential. It gives a boost to your sense of your own power and authority. The true possibility of individual creative expression is often suppressed because of the power and authority which you have invested in others. Until this is withdrawn and reclaimed for yourself, your expression is limited.

Use this remedy whenever there seem to be blockages in personal power and creativity. When inner or outer critics are dominant. Use to gain self-knowledge, freedom of expression and courage to follow your own way of being and doing.

Affirmation

'I am my own authority'

Snapdragon

Keywords: Emotional expression, Confidence, Voice.

A great and very specific essence for anything to do with the voice. Encourages a loosening and outward movement from the throat. For clear and confident vocal expression.

The muscles around the jaw hold a lot of tension. Relaxing them help any public speaking, voice work, singing or speech difficulty. Loosening of the facial muscles also enables emotions and repressed feelings to arise and be expressed. To move you on from frustration, irritation, anger, fear or sadness stuck in the throat or held in the lips and jaw. Extremely useful for adults and children whose small voices need to be heard or babies who are teething.

Affirmation
'I express myself clearly and boldly. All my feelings are valid'.

CD's

Archangelic Guidance
Voice **I**nner Healing **V**ibration with the **A**rchangels.

Patricia Iris focuses you and your intention on inner harmony, using your voice. Experience the power of sound and vibration, meditation and visualisation. A powerful recipe for the 21st century.

Archangelic Blessings
Available in October 2007.

VIVA VOCE
This CD contains the remaining meditations and visualisations contained in this book that are not included in the attached CD. It is available on line for £8.00 plus post and packaging.

Viva Voce – The Living Voice

Medicine Woman
Freefall Soul Music by Patricia Iris and John Sinclair.
Deeply healing, this emotional journey takes you to the heart of Mother Earth. For use as a facilitator of self discovery and bringer of harmony and peace. Available online for £5.00 plus post and packaging.

Books

Viva voce

Free Downloads on www.patriciairis.com

Japa Meditation

Workshops

You can book workshops, courses and sessions on line using Paypal.

Recommended Reading

You Can Heal Your Life - by Louise L Hay. This and all her other best selling titles available from www.hayhouse.co.uk

Goddesses and Angels - by Dr. Doreen Virtue. This and many other books and sets of cards available from www.hayhouse.co.uk

The Power of Intention - by Dr. Wayne W. Dyer.
This and his many other inspirational books available from www.hayhouse .co.uk

Commitment to Love - by Maureen Moss from www.maureen@maureenmoss.com

The True Power of Water - by Masaru Emoto
www.beyondword.com

Power Vs Force - by Dr. David R. Hawkins M.D., PH.D.
www.hayhouse.com

Its the Thought that Counts - by Dr. David Hamilton
www.hayhouse.com

8 Kerinsian Keys to Self Empowerment - by Bill Kerins, Dip CAH ACPAMT. www.billkerins.com

Notes